D1559355

TWO GODS IN HEAVEN

Two Gods in Heaven

JEWISH CONCEPTS OF GOD
IN ANTIQUITY

PETER SCHÄFER

TRANSLATED BY ALLISON BROWN

PRINCETON UNIVERSITY PRESS

PRINCETON & OXFORD

Published by Princeton University Press
41 William Street, Princeton, New Jersey 08540
6 Oxford Street, Woodstock, Oxfordshire OX20 1TR

press.princeton.edu

Library of Congress Cataloging-in-Publication Data

Schäfer, Peter, 1943– author.
Two gods in heaven : Jewish concepts of God in antiquity / Peter Schäfer ; translated by Allison Brown.
Other titles: Zwei Götter im Himmel. English.
LCCN 2019036470 (print) | LCCN 2019036471 (ebook) |
  ISBN 9780691181325 (hardback) | ISBN 9780691199894 (ebook)
LCSH: God (Judaism)—History of doctrines. | Son of God (Judaism) |
  Monotheism. | Christianity and other religions—Judaism.
LCC BM610 .S31613 2020 (print) | LCC BM610 (ebook) | DDC
  296.3/1109—dc23
LC record available at https://lccn.loc.gov/2019036470
LC ebook record available at https://lccn.loc.gov/2019036471

British Library Cataloging-in-Publication Data is available

Original German edition, *Zwei Götter im Himmel*, © Verlag C. H. Beck, 2017.

This book has been composed in Arno

Printed on acid-free paper ∞

Printed in the United States of America

10 9 8 7 6 5 4 3 2 1

CONTENTS

TWO GODS IN HEAVEN

One God?

AMONG THE MOST POPULAR clichés not only in Jewish and Christian theology but also in popular religious belief is the assumption that Judaism is the classic religion of monotheism, and if Judaism did not in fact invent monotheism, then it at least ultimately asserted it.[1] Nothing summarizes this basic assumption better than the affirmation in Deuteronomy 6:4: "Hear, O Israel: The Lord is our God, the Lord is one." As the *Shema' Yisrael*, it became the solemn daily prayer, with which many Jewish martyrs went to their death. Christianity, as this narrative continues, adopted this Jewish monotheism, but quickly expanded it with the idea of the incarnation of God's son, the Logos, and finally watered it down entirely with the doctrine of three divine persons, the Trinity. In this view, Judaism was thus compelled to limit itself even more to the abstract concept of the one and only God. This God could then easily degenerate into the caricature of the Old Covenant's God, who receded ever farther into the distance and against whom the message of the New Covenant could set itself apart with all the more radiance. Judaism, according to this narrative, had no alternative but to assume its assigned role, as there was never a serious, much less balanced dialogue between mother and daughter religion.

We know today that pretty much none of this ideal picture stands up to historical review.[2] Some potential objections have meanwhile become generally accepted, while others are still extremely controversial and the subject of heated discussion. With respect to biblical monotheism, today it can be read in all the related handbooks that this tends to be an ideal type in religious history rather than a historically verifiable reality.[3] The term "monotheism" is a modern coinage, first documented in 1660 by the English philosopher Henry More, who used it to characterize the ideal pinnacle of faith in God. Well into the twentieth century the term continued to play a key role in two opposing models of development of religions: either monotheism was considered the unsurpassable end point in a long chain of religions, which at the dawn of time began with all kinds of "primitive" forms, in order then to be spiritualized in increasingly "pure" forms (the evolutionary model), or on the contrary, it was the original ideal form of religion, which over time continued to degenerate and ultimately lost itself in polytheistic diversity (the decadence model). Both models have long since become obsolete in religious history. Monotheism is neither at the beginning of "religion" nor does it represent the final apex of a linear development. What makes more sense is a dynamic model that dispenses with value judgments, and moves between the two poles of "monotheism" and "polytheism," including numerous configurations and combinations that crystallized at different times and in different geographic regions.

This also means that Jewish monotheism was not "achieved" at a certain point in time in the history of the Hebrew Bible,* in order thereafter only to be defended against attacks from "the outside." This linear developmental model is also outdated. Bible scholars today paint a multifaceted picture of the idea of God in ancient Israel, in which various gods stand side by side and compete with one another. Israel's own God YHWH** had to assert

---

* The term "Hebrew Bible" refers to the Jewish canon of biblical books as opposed to the Christian canon of the "Old Testament."

** The four consonants (the tetragrammaton) forming the name of God, which cannot be uttered.

himself not only against numerous powerful spirits and demons but especially also against the deities of the Ugaritic and Canaanite pantheon, headed by the old god El and his subordinate, the young war god Ba'al. The strategy of the authors and editors of the Hebrew Bible to let competing gods be subsumed in YHWH was not always successful.[4] Ba'al worshippers proved to be particularly resistant to this, as shown by the confrontation of the prophet Elijah against the cult of Ba'al, as demanded by King Ahab in the ninth century BCE (1 Kings 18). The prophet Hosea still felt compelled in the eighth century BCE to take action against the Ba'al worship at the land's high places (Hos. 2).

The ideal of biblical monotheism becomes utterly problematic if we take into account how easily a consort was long associated with the biblical God. The inscriptions of Kuntillet Ajrud near the road from Gaza to Eilat, from the time of the Kingdom of Judah, mention YHWH as the God of Israel together with his Asherah.[5] This Asherah is a well-known Canaanite goddess, also documented in the Bible as the wife of Ba'al (1 Kings 18:19). Her cultic image was worshipped in the Kingdoms of Judah and Israel, and was even displayed by King Manasseh in the YHWH Temple in Jerusalem.[6] The biblical narratives that report triumphantly of the successful destruction of these idols cannot conceal the fact that this cult continued to be widespread, and was revived time and again. Even regarding the fifth century BCE, we hear of Jewish mercenaries who settled in the Egyptian border fortress Elephantine and not only built their own temple there (despite the allegedly one-and-only sanctuary in Jerusalem) but in addition to their God Yahu (YHW), also worshipped two goddesses—and this continued for more than two hundred years without the Temple congregation in Jerusalem being able or inclined to take action against it.

The conflict between a theology that wished to acknowledge only YHWH as God and a religious tradition with many goddesses and gods came to a head in the crisis triggered by the Babylonian exile. While the "angel of the Lord" (Exod. 23:20–33), who is in competition with YHWH and would play a large role in rabbinic commentaries, has been placed by Bible scholarship in an earlier layer in the Hebrew Bible, the indefinite plural in the first story of creation—"Then God said, 'Let *us* make humankind in *our* image, according to *our* likeness" (Gen. 1:26)—is part of the priestly account, which was probably written during the exile. For this reason, the priestly account of creation may well imply a "monotheistic confession,"[7] despite the use of a plural from the mouth of the same God, but this confession, as the rabbis experienced during the confrontation with their Christian, Gnostic, or also inner-Jewish opponents, was anything but uncontested. The same is true for the apocalyptic as well as the wisdom literature of postexilic Judaism of the Second Temple, both belonging to the canonical and especially also noncanonical literature, which will be the subject of the first part of this book. This is not simply a matter of an angelology, which places itself, as a "buffer" as it were, between the ostensible "distance of a God becoming increasingly transcendent" and his earthly people, Israel,[8] yet more directly and tangibly, it is about the return of not many but at least two gods in the Jewish heaven.

No less problematic about the ideal picture sketched above are the roles assigned to Christianity and the rabbinic Judaism* that was becoming established at the same time. There is no doubt that the Christianity of the New Testament and the early church fathers of the first centuries CE adopted Jewish monotheism—however, it was not a "pure" monotheism matured to eternal perfection but rather the "monotheism" that had developed in the postexilic period in the later canonical literature of the Hebrew Bible and noncanonical writings, the so-called apocrypha** and

---

* Rabbinic Judaism is the form of Judaism that developed under the leadership of the rabbis after the destruction of the Second Temple in 70 CE and continued up to the Arab conquest of Palestine in the first half of the seventh century.

** Apocrypha are books that were not included in the canon of the Hebrew Bible or the Christian Old Testament.

pseudepigrapha.* The New Testament took up these traditions that existed in Judaism, and did not reinvent but instead expanded and deepened them. The elevation of Jesus of Nazareth as the first-born before all creation, the God incarnate, Son of God, Son of Man, the Messiah: all these basic Christological premises are not pagan or other kinds of aberrations; they are rooted in Second Temple Judaism, regardless of their specifically Christian character. This is not changed by the fact that the divine duality of father and son led, far beyond the New Testament, to the Trinity of Father, Son, and Holy Spirit, which would then be codified in the First Councils of Nicaea (325 CE) and Constantinople (381 CE).

The Christological and then also the Trinitarian intensification of the concept of God in Christianity by no means implies that rabbinic Judaism forgot or repressed its own roots in Second Temple Judaism. Quite to the contrary. Recent research shows with increasing clarity that the Judaism of the first century CE did not ossify in lonely isolation and self-sufficiency; rather, only through constant discourse with the evolving Christianity did it become what we refer to today as rabbinic Judaism and the Judaism of early Jewish mysticism. Just as Christianity emerged through recourse to and controversy with Judaism, so too the Judaism of the period following the destruction of the Second Temple was not a Judaism identical to that of its early precursors but instead developed in dialogue and controversy with Christianity. Therefore, I prefer to define the relationship between Judaism and Christianity not as linear from the mother to the daughter religion but rather as a dynamic, lively exchange between two sister religions—a process in which the delimitation tendencies steadily grew, leading ultimately to the separation of the two religions. The second part of this book is devoted to this dialectic process of exchange and delimitation.

---

* Pseudepigrapha are noncanonical writings that were (falsely) attributed to a biblical author in order to guarantee or increase their authority.

The title of this examination, *Two Gods in Heaven*, is pointedly based on the rabbinic phrase "two powers in heaven" (*shetei rashuyyot*), which clearly implies two divine authorities side by side. This does not refer to two gods who fight each other in a dualistic sense ("good god" versus "evil god"), as we are familiar with primarily from Gnosticism, but rather two gods who rule side by side and together—in different degrees of agreement and correlation. Scholarship has developed the term "binitarian" to describe this juxtaposition of two powers or gods, analogous to the term "trinitarian" associated with Christian dogma.[9]

The theme of two divine authorities in the Jewish heaven is not new. Almost all pertinent studies follow the key rabbinic concept of "two powers," concentrating on the period of classical rabbinic Judaism. After the pioneering work of R. Travers Herford, the revised dissertation of Alan Segal, *Two Powers in Heaven*, is considered a milestone in more recent research.[10] Despite their indisputable merits, however, both works set out from the premise that the rabbis, in their polemics against "two powers," were referring to clearly identifiable "heretic sects" that were beginning to break off from "orthodox" Judaism. For Herford, it was overwhelmingly Christianity that incurred the wrath of the rabbis, whereas Segal attempted to address an entire spectrum of pagans, Christians, Jewish Christians, and Gnostics. But ultimately, even Segal's *Two Powers in Heaven* remains caught in the methodological straitjacket of dogmatically established "religions" that defended themselves against "sects" and "heresies."

Since then, the binitarian traditions of ancient Judaism have increasingly moved into the spotlight of research, though with different premises for early and rabbinic Judaism. Research in the field of Jewish studies continues to concentrate primarily on the rabbinic Judaism that was gradually emerging and its confrontation with nascent Christianity. The programmatic works of Daniel Boyarin have pride of place here. With his book *Border Lines: The Partition of Judaeo-Christianity*[11] and an impressive series of articles,[12] Boyarin attempted to break down the rigid fronts of "Christianity" versus "Judaism" and "orthodoxy" versus "heresy" in favor of a more differentiated picture, according to which the rabbis were not (yet) fighting against external enemies, but were arguing primarily with opponents within their own rabbinic movement. I have joined the discussion with my books *Die Geburt des Judentums aus dem Geist des Christentums* (The Birth of Judaism out of the Spirit of Christianity) and *The Jewish Jesus: How Judaism and Christianity Shaped Each Other*, and in recent years, this conversation has been carried on predominantly between Boyarin and myself.[13] In 2012 and 2013, Menahem Kister added two articles to the debate that are as significant as they are comprehensive, but that unfortunately exist up to now only in Hebrew.[14] Kister again invokes the old static model of "Judaism" and "Christianity" as two religions that were permanently separated early on, claiming that in contrast to the Christians, who were driven by theological questions, the rabbis were concerned "only" with solving exegetical problems that arose from contradictory Bible verses. Accordingly, binitarian ideas in Judaism were a construct of modern research and thus never considered by the rabbis.

Early Judaism—that is, the period *prior* to rabbinic Judaism and the New Testament—has up to now been examined predominantly by Christian New Testament scholars. With his seminal contribution on the Son of God, Martin Hengel opened up an entire field of research that has since gained considerable influence especially in Anglo-Saxon research under the heading of "High Christology."[15] "High Christology" is understood as referring to the Christology of the New Testament that specifically addresses the divinity of Jesus, in contrast to "Low Christology," which is primarily concerned with Jesus's human nature. If the writings of the New Testament—that is, long before the later dogmatic statements by the church fathers—already speak of the idea of Jesus's divinity and his being worshipped as a second God next to God the Father (which is generally affirmed), how does this relate to the supposed biblical and early Jewish monotheism?

Diverse research literature has meanwhile emerged on this, covering the range between these two poles:[16] from, on the one hand, advocates of an exclusive monotheism who view early Judaism as bearing witness only to a strict belief in the one and only God, through, on the other hand, all possible stages of an inclusive and fluid monotheism up to authors who recognize authentic early Judaism in the idea of two Gods side by side.[17] The assessment of the divinity of Jesus then results from its relation to the varying degrees of early Jewish monotheism: almost all authors, including the exclusive monotheists, meanwhile concede that numerous mediator figures (angels, patriarchs, personified divine attributes, etc.) were known to early Judaism, but they remain at the level of divine agents and do not explain the undisputed divinity of Jesus. The latter results, as Larry Hurtado has stated with particular emphasis, exclusively from the cultic worship and veneration of Jesus, which is what comprises the "binitarian mutation" in Jewish monotheism that is characteristic of early Christianity. According to Richard Bauckham, a contemporary ally of Hurtado, the ostensibly strict early Jewish monotheism can only be overcome when Jesus becomes identical with the one and only Jewish God.[18] The messiah Jesus is not a second semidivine figure but instead God himself. This is without doubt the most radical deduction from an extreme Jewish monotheism.[19]

A few years ago, Boyarin attempted with his book *The Jewish Gospels: The Story of the Jewish Christ* to supplement his works on rabbinic Judaism by including early Jewish literature from the Hebrew Bible up to New Testament Christianity.[20] In my review of this book, I drew attention to the copious postexilic literature on our topic, which has not yet received sufficient attention, not even by Boyarin.[21] With the present book, I would like to venture to bring together the two eras and for the first time focus on ancient Judaism in its entirety from the Hebrew Bible to the end of the rabbinic period—that is, the Second Temple period or early Judaism *and* rabbinic Judaism. In doing this, I expressly do not wish to get involved in the sophisticated New Testament discussion on the divinity of Jesus and its roots in early Judaism, but it will certainly not hurt if my considerations from a strictly Jewish studies perspective are heard in this to some degree very heated debate.[22] My integration of early Jewish mysticism on equal terms with classical rabbinic Judaism gives this book a particular focus.

Accordingly, the book is divided into two parts. The first part, on "Second Temple Judaism," starts with the Son of Man in the Book of Daniel, which determines a great share of the subsequent discussion. He can likely be interpreted as the angel Michael, the divine representative of the people Israel, who anticipates in heaven the expected earthly victory of Israel over the pagan nations. With him, for the first time an angel enters the scene who is elevated to quasi godlike status, and in this capacity, represents in heaven the interests of God's earthly people. This is followed by a chapter on the wisdom literature, as reflected in the canonical Proverbs and noncanonical books Jesus Sirach (Ecclesiasticus) and Wisdom of Solomon (Sapientia Salomonis). Here two competing strands of tradition become visible—namely, first a strand that is traditionally biblical, according to which wisdom was created as a child (more precisely, a daughter) of God prior to the creation of the world, initially enthroned with God in heaven, and then sent as his envoy to humankind (more precisely, the people Israel) on earth. The second strand, which is largely influenced by Platonic philosophy, regards wisdom as the archetype of divine perfection that imparts divine strength to the earthly world in various stages of emanation. In Judaism, this became the Torah; in Christianity, it became the personified Logos.

The next two chapters deal with two texts of the Qumran community, both of which further develop the theme of the divinization of an angel or human being, as laid out in Daniel. Whereas Daniel does not clarify the origin of the "Son of Man," in the first text, the so-called self-glorification hymn, for the first time it is clearly a human being who appears and is elevated to heaven in a previously unheard-of manner, and is then enthroned there as a divine-messianic figure among and above the angels. The second text, the so-called Apocryphon of Daniel, is an interpretation of the biblical Book of Daniel. It raises the "Son of Man" of Daniel 7 to the "Son of God" and "Son of the Most High," expecting from him the eschatological redemption of the people Israel.

Two chapters follow on key themes of the so-called Pseudepigrapha of the Hebrew Bible. The first is dedicated to the Similitudes of the Ethiopian Book of Enoch, in which the Son of Man, who is seated on the throne of God's glory as an eschatological judge, is none other than Enoch, the human being elevated into heaven. The second deals with the Fourth Book of Ezra's Son of Man, who is equated with the Messiah, and thus will conquer the pagan nations at the end of time and reveal himself to be the "Son of God." We can observe in these texts the two opposing—or more precisely, the constantly overlapping—lines from an angel who is elevated to a divine or semidivine figure, and who will appear at the end of time as the redeemer of Israel, and that of an immortal human being who ascends into heaven, and once there, transformed into an angel, takes his place as a virtually godlike figure of redemption.

The two final chapters in the first part pursue the philosophically informed theme of the wisdom literature. In the Prayer of Joseph, the highest angel Israel, as the firstborn before all creation, is identical with the human Jacob, patriarch of Israel. The highest angel in heaven is hence in reality a human being, who as the sole creature was with God in heaven prior to all creation. The role of wisdom in the canonical and noncanonical books of the Bible is now assumed by a human being who, however, does not need to be transformed into an angel, but from the very beginning is equated with a human being: the angel is a human being, and the human being is an angel. The parallels to the godlike Jesus Christ, who as the firstborn before all creation was always with God, but who had to assume human form in order to complete the divine work of redemption, are obvious. For the Jewish philosopher Philo, it is the Logos, the creative power of God, who is not only characterized as the firstborn before all creation and highest among the angels but also as the archetypal human being created in the image of God. It is virtually impossible to get any closer to the idea of two gods in heaven, and it is hardly surprising that Philo's later Christian followers elevated him to the status of the church fathers.

The second part of the book, "Rabbinic Judaism and Early Jewish Mysticism," offers for the first time an analysis of the different strands of classical rabbinic literature in a narrower sense and early Jewish mysticism in a combined context. Striking differences become apparent between rabbinic Judaism in Palestine, on the one hand, and Babylonian rabbinic Judaism and Jewish mysticism, on the other. The first chapter, devoted to the continuation of the Son of Man tradition in rabbinic Judaism, comes to the conclusion that the Son of Man is virtually irrelevant among the rabbis of Palestine, in contrast to the Second Temple period. Essentially, only one Palestinian midrash* is cited in research (a commentary to the Bible verse Exod. 20:2), in which the different guises of God as an older and younger God are discussed. Since the Bible verse Daniel 7:9, which plays a central role in the Babylonian Talmud (see chapter 9), appears in the context of this discussion, some scholars regard this midrash as early evidence for the continuation of binitarian traditions in Palestinian rabbinic Judaism. My analysis of the midrash comes to a different conclusion. I do not see any evidence in the sources of Palestinian Judaism for the Son of God as a second deity next to the biblical God of creation, and I presume that the usurpation of the Jewish Son of Man by the New Testament—Jesus as the Son of Man who will come with the clouds of heaven and is enthroned at the right hand of God[23]—served to prevent the reception and further development of this originally elementary Jewish idea in the Judaism of the increasingly Christianizing Palestine.

---

* "Midrash" (plural "midrashim") is the technical term for both individual interpretations of the Hebrew Bible in classical rabbinic literature and the collected works devoted to the respective books of the Bible.

The situation is different with respect to Babylonian Judaism (see chapter 10). There, Christianity played only a subordinate role, and it was precisely there that binitarian ideas survived. It is the Babylonian Talmud (and not a Palestinian source) that identifies the Messiah-King David with the Son of Man of Daniel and lets him sit on a throne next to God. And it is none other than Rabbi Aqiva, one of the heroes of both rabbinic Judaism and early Jewish mysticism,[24] who is said to have uttered this equation— and is immediately and passionately contradicted by his rabbinic colleagues. Here we are encountering for the first time a pattern that will pass through almost all relevant sources of this epoch: namely, the renewal of bold binitarian thoughts in certain *Jewish* circles in Babylonia and the refutation of these ideas as well as harsh polemics against them in mainstream rabbinic Jewish society. While the Babylonian Talmud presents the elevation of David as a divinized Son of Man only together with polemics against it, the Hekhalot literature, the literature of early Jewish mysticism,* is much more impartial: for the David Apocalypse, which appears only in the Hekhalot literature, it is completely undisputed that David is the Messiah-King who was elevated into heaven and enthroned next to God. Christian parallels in the Apocalypse of John (Revelation) in the New Testament as well as those expressed by the church fathers Ephrem the Syrian and John Chrysostom show why most Babylonian rabbis reacted so aversely to the elevation of David as a godlike Son of Man and Messiah-King.

Precisely this pattern can also be observed in the traditions surrounding the patriarch Enoch, which were also taken up and

---

* Hekhalot literature refers to the sources dealing with the *hekhalot*, the heavenly "halls" or "palaces" that mystics pass through on their journey to heaven, in order to reach the divine throne (*merkavah*) in the seventh "palace"; these "halls" or "palaces" can also be equated with the seven heavens. The term *hekhal* in the singular originally comes from the architecture of the earthly Temple, where it is used specifically for the main sanctuary in front of the Holy of Holies. The mystic who embarks on the heavenly ascent is paradoxically called *yored merkavah*, which literally means the one who "descends" to the Merkavah.

further pursued in rabbinic Judaism and early Jewish mysticism (see chapter 11). Here too, similar to the Son of Man, it is striking that the Palestinian rabbinic sources are reserved and tend to express a negative connotation, whereas the Babylonian rabbinic sources and the Hekhalot literature again reveal the ambivalence of adoption and rejection. After a short survey of the figure of Enoch—the only antediluvian patriarch who did not die a natural death but instead was received alive in heaven—in the Hebrew Bible and the apocryphal Books of Enoch, I will analyze the only Palestinian midrash that discusses Enoch's fate. Only here do we encounter a rejection of Enoch's ascension to heaven in a polemic whose harshness is virtually unparalleled. The Palestinian rabbis, in marked contrast to their early Jewish colleagues during the Second Temple period, considered Enoch evil. They felt not only that he died a natural death but also that he deserved it. Looking at the contemporary Christian sources that take up the pre-Christian Jewish line of tradition and reinterpret it in a Christian sense, it becomes immediately obvious why the Palestinian rabbis reacted as they did.

Early Jewish mysticism responded in a very different way. In the Third Book of Enoch, the latest of the Hekhalot literature, the human Enoch is transformed into the highest angel Metatron and given the honorific title "Younger" or "Lesser God" (*YHWH ha-qatan*). This represents the pinnacle of binitarian traditions in late antique Judaism. How dangerous these thoughts could be viewed is demonstrated in the midrash on the ascent of Elisha ben Avuyah to the seventh heaven, where he sees Metatron sitting on a divine throne and concludes from this that there must be "two powers" in heaven, God and Metatron—an insight that is interpreted as heresy, bringing with it the immediate punishment of both the rabbi and Metatron. Here too the tone in the Hekhalot literature is much more reserved than in the parallel account in the Babylonian Talmud.

The same applies to the complex of traditions surrounding Akatriel, an angel who is identical with Metatron. Whereas in the

Hekhalot literature it is not the rabbi but rather God himself who becomes the protagonist of a second divine being at his side, it is once again the Babylonian Talmud that adjusts the standards in a parallel version, reestablishing the "pure doctrine" of the one and only God. This pattern is repeated in the final source on Rav Idith and Metatron. In a midrash that appears only in the Babylonian Talmud, the rabbi and an unknown heretic argue over Metatron; the rabbi imprudently admits that Metatron has the same name as God, thereby inadvertently representing the notion of a second God—which the horrified rabbi then awkwardly denies. Thus the Talmud again attempts to use polemics to defuse the binitarian idea. Here too, texts from the Hekhalot literature that have been largely neglected up to now offer evidence that within the circles of Jewish mystics, the idea of two Gods in heaven had become established, which is why it was so harshly opposed by the rabbis of the Babylonian Talmud.

This completes the outline of the notion of two Gods in the Jewish heaven, from the biblical Book of Daniel to rabbinic Judaism and the Jewish mysticism of late antiquity. In terms of methodology, I have chosen not to put forward any general overview or lofty theories but instead to develop my ideas from the respective sources. Thus I ask readers to bear with me in my interpretation of some key texts, as there is no other credible way for me to approach this difficult subject with such far-reaching consequences. Essentially, I assert nothing less than that the idea of a triumphant monotheism cannot be maintained for postexilic Judaism after Daniel, let alone for post–New Testament Judaism. Late antique Judaism was itself susceptible to binitarian thought, regardless of all efforts to separate it from Christianity. This applies first and foremost to the protagonists of early Jewish mysticism, who were by no means confined to hermetically sealed and obscure circles, but made their way into the center of Babylonian rabbinic Judaism. Despite the usurpation of binitarian ideas by New Testament Christology and early Christian authors, rabbinic Judaism and the Judaism of the early mystics held firm to these ideas. By reviving the idea of two Gods in the Jewish heaven, late antique Judaism was also responding to Christianity's claims, but this response was in essence genuinely Jewish, and as such, not only defensive and delimiting, but affirmative as well. To this extent, early Christianity and rabbinic Judaism were also competing for the second God beside God the Creator.

PART I

Second Temple Judaism

SECOND TEMPLE JUDAISM roughly covers Judaism in the period following the return from Babylonian exile, that is, from the rebuilding of the First Temple around 515 BCE, after it had been destroyed in 586 BCE, until the ultimate destruction of this so-called Second Temple by the Romans in 70 CE. The Second Temple had been plundered and desecrated in 169 BCE under Antiochus IV, and then retaken and rededicated by the Maccabees. In 20 BCE, King Herod began the renovation and new construction of this temple, which was not completed until 64 CE, shortly before it was destroyed by the Romans. The term "Second Temple Judaism," which is common especially in Hebrew, highlights the significance of the temple cult for the politics, religion, and culture of Judaism of this era, as reflected in all the relevant literature. The German term *Frühjudentum* (early Judaism) emerged to counter the term *Spätjudentum* (late Judaism) for the period of rabbinic Judaism in the first centuries of the Common Era, which for good reason has meanwhile fallen out of use.

The literature of the Second Temple period is very diverse, and reflects numerous, different, and often-controversial orientations of postexilic Judaism. The dominant—and thus for our purposes, key—trend can be characterized as apocalyptic, that is, revolving around the anticipation of the end of days and the final redemption of the people of Israel in the struggle against the godless powers of pagan nations threatening Israel. A trend that should be clearly distinguished from this—which also reflects our subject— is the wisdom tradition stemming from the religious culture around Israel, in particular from Egypt, which would reach its peak in the idea of Logos as a divine emanation.

1

The Son of Man
in the Vision of Daniel

THE POINT OF DEPARTURE of all binitarian speculations in Judaism is the enigmatic "Son of Man" in the biblical Book of Daniel. This book consists of various parts that were written at different times. It is certain that its final editing took place during the Maccabean period—that is, in the first half of the second century BCE. Four visions of Daniel are described in chapters 7 through 12 of that book; the key vision for our context is that of the four beasts and the one like a human being, or Son of Man, in chapter 7.

Let me briefly recount what happens in the vision in Daniel 7:9ff. Daniel sees that thrones are being set in place in heaven and an "Ancient One / Ancient of Days," obviously God, takes his seat (Dan. 7:9). This is embedded in a vision of four beasts—a lion, bear, leopard, and fourth beast not identified more precisely, but a particularly terrifying one with ten horns and one extra horn. Directly after the Ancient One takes his place, the court sits in judgment, books are opened (v. 10), and the beasts are judged (v. 11–12). Then Daniel sees "one like the son of a man" (*ke-var enash*), coming with the clouds of heaven (v. 13). This is the notorious Son of Man in the Book of Daniel, whereby "son of a man" is an overly literal mistranslation of the Aramaic *bar enash* (*ben adam* in Hebrew); more accurate would be "someone who looks like a human being." This marks the beginning of the long career of this Son of Man, which finally leads into the New Testament. The "human being"[1] is presented in Daniel to the Ancient One, and given "dominion and glory and kingship" (v. 14) forever. Here are the critical verses in context:

> (Dan. 7:9) I watched until thrones were set in place, and an Ancient of Days (*'atiq yomin*) took his seat; his clothing was white as snow, and the hair of his head like pure wool; his throne was fiery flames, and its wheels were burning fire.
>
> (10) A river of fire issued and came forth from before him. Thousands upon thousands served him, and myriads upon myriads stood attending him. The court sat in judgment, and the books were opened....
>
> (13) As I watched in the night visions, I saw one like a human being coming with the clouds of heaven. And he came to the Ancient One and was presented before him.
>
> (14) To him was given dominion and glory and kingship; all peoples, nations, and languages should serve him. His dominion is an everlasting dominion that shall not pass away, and his kingship is one that shall never be destroyed.

This vision is supplemented by an interpretation (*peshar*) by the biblical author. The beasts are four earthly kings, but the *qaddishe 'elyonin,* usually translated as the "holy ones of the Most High," will receive and possess the kingdom forever and ever (v. 18). The additional horn of the particularly terrifying fourth beast will make war with the holy ones (*qaddishin*), until the Ancient One comes and judgment is passed on the holy ones of the Most High (v. 22). The fourth beast is interpreted to mean the fourth kingdom; his ten horns are ten kings, and the additional, eleventh horn is another king (obviously the Seleucid King Antiochus IV Epiphanes), the worst of all, who speaks arrogantly against God (v. 20) and makes war with the holy ones (v. 21). He will change their sacred seasons and law for a time (v. 25), but his rule is limited: his dominion will be taken away (v. 26) and given as an ever-lasting kingdom to the people of the holy ones of the Most High ('am qaddishe 'elyonin) (v. 27).

But who exactly is the Ancient One, who is the "one like a human being," and who are the holy ones of the Most High? Regarding the first two questions, the Ancient One and the "one like a human being," it has long since been noted that there is a striking similarity to the Canaanite Pantheon: El as the highest "father god," and Ba'al as the young warrior god, who rides on a cloud chariot.[2] Following this, Daniel Boyarin explains the Daniel vision as a version of this old myth, which transforms the Canaanite God El into Israel's God YHWH and the "one like a human being" into a second, as yet nameless divinity subordinate to the highest God YHWH; the former is an old God, and the latter is a young, aspiring, and ambitious God.[3] In contrast to Boyarin, Michael Segal comes to the conclusion in his book on Daniel—confirmed through a careful analysis of the relevant biblical and nonbiblical parallels—that the Ancient One is indeed El.[4] Yet it is not the Ancient One but rather the "one like a human being" who is equated with YHWH as the second divine figure, subordinate to El.[5] Finally, with respect to the phrase "holy ones of the Most High," qaddishe 'elyonin, most exegetes interpret the plural 'elyonin as a grammatical plural to refer to God, but with a singular meaning (like elohim),* that is, "the holy ones of the Most High (God)," whereby the "holy ones" can be understood to mean either the angels or the people of Israel (the latter is supported by the phrase "the people of the holy ones of the Most High" in verse 27).[6] Segal's bold argument against this traditional interpretation understands qaddishe 'elyonin not as "the holy ones of the Most High" but rather as the "most high holy one" to be identified as YHWH, the second divine figure in the vision. This yields a direct correlation

---

* "Elohim," in addition to the tetragrammaton YHWH, is the second name for God used in the Hebrew Bible.

between the "one like a human being" (= YHWH) in the vision and the "most high holy one" (= YHWH) in the interpretation of the vision.

Without wanting to examine the philological details discussed extensively by Segal, I feel this explanation tends to obscure the difference between the vision and its interpretation in the Book of Daniel. In my opinion, vision and interpretation operate at two different levels—namely, in heaven and on earth. The vision refers to heaven, where dominion and kingdom are given to the "one like a human being." The interpretation refers to the earth, where dominion and kingdom are transferred to the people Israel. That which is initially carried out in heaven is finally completed on earth: in other words, the Maccabees defeat the wicked King Antiochus IV Epiphanes. To be sure, vision and interpretation cannot be neatly separated from each other—elements of both overlap, and it is possible that the "one like a human being" in the vision influences the "holy ones" in the interpretation—but the key point of the *peshar* is to transfer to the earthly people of Israel that which first took place in heaven.

This interpretation of the vision and the *peshar* is of direct relevance for the question as to who the "one like a human being" is in the Book of Daniel. Is the dual godhead (El / Ancient One / YHWH and Baʿal / Son of Man, according to Boyarin, or El / Ancient One and YHWH / Son of Man, according to Segal) only the late revival of an old myth, an "echo of its mythical sources" in Segal, or is it the beginning of something entirely new, as Boyarin says: two divine figures, "one apparently old and one apparently young,"[7] whereby the as yet nameless young God will become the redeemer and eternal ruler of the world, leading in a direct line to the messianic Son of Man of the Similitudes in the First Book of Enoch, to Jesus in the New Testament, and to Metatron in the Hekhalot literature. Whereas Segal limits himself convincingly—albeit perhaps a bit too restrictively—to the biblical context, Boyarin goes too far in the opposite direction and actually reads the later development into the biblical Daniel text. He makes much ado in emphasizing that the "one like a human being" is a genuine divine figure and not just a symbol (which most exegetes would not doubt in any case, regardless of his claim to the contrary),[8] and that this second divine figure in the vision is enthroned on a second throne next to God's throne in heaven.[9] Unfortunately, however, the Daniel text does not mention Boyarin's desired *two* thrones but instead only unspecified "thrones" (in plural), and the obvious, literal sense of these thrones is that one throne is reserved for the Ancient One and the other thrones are meant for the heavenly court, of which verse 10 explicitly says that it "sat in judgment." Boyarin's two thrones—one for the old God and the other for the young Son of Man—are evidently inspired by Rabbi Aqiva's famous exegesis of the plural thrones in the Babylonian Talmud, which I discuss later in greater detail.[10]

There can be no doubt that without the later tradition history, which Boyarin reads into the vision of Daniel, we would find neither two thrones in Daniel nor the enthronization of the Son of Man next to God in heaven.[11] The "one like a human being," the Son of Man, disappears in Daniel as suddenly as he appeared, and we do not know what happened to him. Nevertheless, it would be wrong to be content with reading Daniel's vision exclusively within its biblical context and interpret it only from this inner-biblical context. We cannot rule out that something is introduced in the Book of Daniel that goes beyond the ancient Canaanite myth in its new biblical form (Daniel), which was so convincingly reconstructed by Segal—something that opens up the possibilities in the Book of Daniel itself that then unfolds more concretely in the later developments.[12]

This will become clearer if we adopt the identification of the Son of Man with the archangel Michael.[13] This yields complete correspondence between the people of the holy ones of the Most High (Israel as an angel-like community) and the "one like a human being" (Michael as the guardian angel of this people). It is certainly no coincidence that the angels in the sections after Daniel 7 are expressly described as human beings—using varied terminology such as "man" (*gaver*), "human being" (*adam*), "human beings" (*bene adam*), and "man" (*ish*)[14]—and thus it makes sense to interpret also the "one like a human being" to be a particularly high angelic being, if not actually as the archangel Michael. Although in Ezekiel 1:26 (and only there), it is God who is described as a figure "that looked like a human being" (*ke-mareh adam*),[15] this certainly is not sufficient proof for the theory that the "one like a human being" in Daniel is no one else but God.[16] Even in the Book of Ezekiel, the expression "a figure that looked like a man" (*ke-mareh ish*)[17] (Ezek. 8:2)—in the same figurative language as in Ezekiel 1—is clearly used for an angel and not God.

I would like to close by putting forward the thesis that it is likely that the "one like a human being" or the Son of Man in Daniel 7 is a highest angelic figure distinct from God, presumably the archangel Michael. Elevated to a godlike status, this angelic figure becomes the origin and point of departure for the later binitarian figures who will reach their culmination and end point in Metatron.

2

The Personified Wisdom in the Wisdom Literature

WITH THE ACCEPTANCE of wisdom (Hebr. *hokhmah*, and Greek *sophia*) as a way of living and proper lifestyle, Second Temple Judaism assumed patterns of thinking and living that were closely tied to related ancient Near Eastern, Egyptian, and Greek ideas, and probably originated among professional scribes and members of the educated elite at the royal court. In the postexilic period, they were reflected in various canonical (Job and Proverbs) and noncanonical books (Jesus Sirach and Wisdom of Solomon). Common to all these books is their highly poetic quality and the fact that they link wisdom with the process of creation. In addition, and this is critical in our context, they view wisdom as a person, specifically a woman, who was created by God before the creation of the earthly world.[1]

The wisdom tradition in the biblical book of Proverbs, which probably goes back to the third century BCE, is an exegetic hornet's nest,[2] and here I will limit myself to explaining my approach, without any major discussion. In the key chapter 8, the personified Wisdom herself announces in multiple poetic attempts that she was created by God prior to the creation of the earthly and heavenly worlds (Prov. 8:22ff.): the Lord "created" (*qanani*) me at the beginning of his work; ages ago I was "set up" (*nassakhti*),[3] when there were no depths and before the mountains had been shaped, before the hills, I was "born" (*holalti*), when he established the heavens, "I was there." And finally (Prov. 8:29–30):

> When he marked out the foundations of the earth,
> then I was beside him, like an *amon*;
> and I was daily his delight,
> playing before him always.

The word *amon* is a hapax legomenon—that is, a term that appears only once in the Hebrew Bible—and it stands at the beginning of a rich exegetic tradition.[4] The two most important interpretations are "masterworker" and "little child"; the former is supported, for example, by the Septuagint, the canonical Greek Bible translation, which speaks of *harmozousa*, "the woman who holds all things together in harmony."[5] The interpretation as "child" can be found in the text of the Greek Bible translator Aquila in the second century CE, who rendered *amon* as *tithēnoumenē*, "nursling, darling child." Owing to the context, I agree with the interpretation as "nursling, darling child," for one thing, because Wisdom was "born" only shortly before the creation of the world, and for another, because she "plays" before God the whole time as God's "joy." Wisdom is clearly understood here as a person, in fact as a small child, or more precisely, a little girl, who is presented in some not specified way as God's child. No matter how such an idea made its way into biblical Judaism—research has correctly pointed to nonbiblical parallels, especially the Egyptian Maat/Isis—it does not correlate entirely with the much-invoked biblical monotheism.[6] Whereas in older biblical books, pagan polytheistic and especially also dualistic ideas of God (such as El and Ba'al) are integrated into the one Jewish God, and thus tempered or (as in the case of Asherah as the consort of El or Ba'al) eliminated, here we are confronted with the quite unbiased attempt to expand the strict unity of the one and undivided God in—to phrase it carefully—familial dimensions.

The noncanonical book Jesus Sirach (Ecclesiasticus) is close to Proverbs both chronologically and in terms of content. Sirach was written around 190 BCE in Hebrew and translated into Greek by the grandson of the author around 132 BCE. Here too Wisdom explains her origins in a solemn first-person narrative:

> (24:3) I came forth from the mouth of the Most High,
> and covered the earth like a mist.
> (4) I dwelt in the highest heavens,
> and my throne was in a pillar of cloud.
> (5) Alone I compassed the vault of heaven
> and traversed the depths of the abyss.
> (6) Over waves of the sea, over all the earth,
> and over every people and nation I have held sway.

And here as well, Wisdom emerged prior to the creation of the world, before the universe had taken on its final form. And here too she is to be understood as a person and even enthroned on a cloud throne in heaven. But in contrast to Proverbs, where it is not explained how she was created, here Wisdom comes forth from the mouth of God, and thus she is obviously God's word—which is nevertheless interpreted as a person, since she lives in heaven, sits on a throne, compasses the heavenly and earthly vaults, and rules over the land, seas, and all peoples. In this quality she is absolutely singular, because at this time no one else exists besides her (and God). Her coming forth from the mouth of God is more reminiscent of the "spirit of God" in Genesis 1:2, which swept over the face of the primordial waters, than of the small child in Proverbs, and hence it suggests an equation of Wisdom with the Logos.

The Wisdom of Solomon, which is also noncanonical, was written in the first century BCE. It continues precisely this tradition of the identification of Wisdom with the Logos. At the beginning of the book, wisdom and (holy) spirit are used virtually synonymously:

> (1:4) Because wisdom will not enter a deceitful soul,
> or dwell in a body enslaved to sin.

(5) For a holy and disciplined spirit will flee from deceit, …
(6) For wisdom is a kindly spirit,
but will not free blasphemers from the guilt of their words.

Here, Wisdom or the holy spirit are gifts from God to the righteous person. Solomon prays for her, and she is bestowed on him as the "spirit of wisdom" (Wisd. of Sol. 7:7). God is the "guide of wisdom" (7:15), and Wisdom is the "fashioner (*technitis*) of all things" (7:21–22). He created all things by his word and humankind by his wisdom (9:1–2). Wisdom and spirit are identical, so one can speak almost paradoxically of wisdom that it *is* spirit and at the same time *possesses* a spirit: "There is in her [Wisdom] a spirit (*esti gar en autē pneuma*) that is intelligent and holy, unique and yet manifold, subtle, mobile, clear" (7:22).

With respect to the essence of wisdom, Wisdom of Solomon maintains the tradition of the personified Wisdom that is presented in Proverbs and Jesus Sirach, on the one hand, and reinforces the philosophical, less personal interpretation of wisdom, on the other. She sits on the throne at God's side (9:4) and was present when he created the world (9:9). At the same time, however, she is

(7:25) a breath[7] of the power of God,
and a pure emanation (*aporroia eilikrinēs*) of the glory of
   the Almighty;
therefore nothing defiled gains entrance into her.
(26) For she is a reflection (*apaugasma*) of eternal light,
a spotless mirror of the working of God (*tēs tou theou
   energeias*),
and an image (*eikōn*) of his goodness.

Wisdom flows from God. In a platonic sense, she is the archetype of his perfection and at the same time his emanation, which imparts God's glory and active workings into the earthly world: "In every generation she passes into holy souls and makes them friends of God, and prophets" (7:27).

Now we have come full circle. Wisdom is (in biblical terms) with God and is enthroned with him, yet at the same time she is identical to him as the platonic archetype, emanating as God's working into the souls of humankind. This drive of Wisdom to be immanent in the earthly world of human beings is—with varied accents—common to all three books of wisdom. In the biblical Book of Proverbs, it is still expressed with reserve, as directly after Wisdom plays before God the text continues somewhat cryptically, "I was playing in his inhabited world, finding delight in humankind" (Prov. 8:31). In Wisdom of Solomon, the drive toward immanence is philosophical, and in Jesus Sirach, it assumes a totally new form. The author of Jesus Sirach lets there be no doubt where the personified wisdom ultimately belongs:

> (24:8) Then the Creator of all things gave me a command,
> and my Creator chose the place for my tent.
> He said, "Make your dwelling in Jacob,
> and in Israel receive your inheritance."

Wisdom, God's little daughter from the biblical Book of Proverbs, thus takes her final residence among the people of Israel, in the holy tent in Zion, as is afterward stated (v. 10), in Jerusalem, God's beloved city (v. 11). Expressed in a different, bolder manner, the incarnated Wisdom is sent by God to the people on earth in order to live among them. But what exactly does it mean that Wisdom lives among the people? The terminology used (holy tent, Zion, and Jerusalem) of course indicates Wisdom's presence in the Temple, but Jesus Sirach does not leave it at this rather traditional idea. The text suddenly takes an unexpected turn:

> (24:23) All this (*tauta panta*) is the book of the covenant
>   (*biblos diathēkēs*) of the Most High God,
> the law (*nomos*) that Moses commanded us
> as an inheritance for the congregations of Jacob.

"All this" refers to everything that had previously been said about wisdom; all this is now interpreted as the Book of the Covenant between God and his people Israel—that is, as the Torah (Greek *nomos*). Wisdom, God's personified messenger on earth, is now embodied in a book, the book of the Torah. This reinterpretation of biblical wisdom paved the way that classical rabbinic Judaism would take: from personified Wisdom to the book of the Torah, which needs to be interpreted. Hence, the so-called Fragment Targum, one of the oldest Palestinian targumim on the Torah,* translates the verse Genesis 1:1 *be-reshit bara Elohim* not as "in the beginning God created the heaven and the earth" but instead as "through/by means of wisdom (*be-hokhmah*)[8] God created and perfected the heaven and the earth."[9] "Wisdom" here of course means "Torah," as explicitly explained in the midrash Genesis Rabbah:[10]

> The Torah declares: *be-reshit* God created [the heaven and the earth] (Gen. 1:1), and *reshit* refers to the Torah, as it is said: "The Lord created me (*qanani*) as the beginning (*reshit*) of his way." (Prov. 8:22)

Here, the *reshit* from Genesis 1:1 is interpreted through Proverbs 8:22. There, Wisdom says of herself that she is the beginning (*reshit*) of his way—that is, his act of creation; accordingly, the *reshit* in Genesis 1:1 must refer to wisdom: *be-reshit* means, as in the targum, "through/by means of wisdom." At the same time we know from Jesus Sirach 24:23 that this wisdom is identical to the Torah, so the verse Genesis 1:1 according to this rabbinic interpretation means "through/by means of *the Torah* God created the heavens and the earth." Thus in contrast to the canonical and noncanonical wisdom tradition, the Torah is not only the first created work of creation but also God's tool of creation. As a parable in the midrash further expounds, God looked in the Torah while creating the world—that is, he used it as a blueprint as it were for his creation. In contrast to this, New Testament Christi-

---

* The term "targum" (plural "targumim") refers to the Aramaic translations of the Hebrew Bible in late antiquity that were completed in various time periods.

anity continues the line of the personified (male) Logos, referring it to Jesus: "In the beginning was the Word, and the Word was with God, and the Word was God" (John 1:1).

This Christological interpretation can be found, of all places, in the oldest complete Palestinian targum on the Pentateuch that we know of: the so-called Codex Neofiti. In the Aramaic translation of the Codex Neofiti, Genesis 1:1 reads, *Mileqadmin behokhmah bera de-YYY' shakhlel yat shemayya we-yat ar'a*,[11] which can only be translated literally as, "In the beginning, by means of wisdom, the son of God perfected the heaven and the earth." This version combines the two variants of the Fragment Targum (*mileqadmin*, "in/at the beginning," and *be-hokhmah*, "through/by means of wisdom"), and by inserting the particle "*de*" before *YYY'*, transforms the verb *bera* (created) into the noun *bera* (son): "the son of God/God's son." Since the verb *bera* was no longer there and *shakhlel* (perfected) remained as the only verb, the copula *we-* (and) before *shakhlel* (also in the Fragment Targum) no longer made sense and was deleted by a redactor, as can easily be seen on a photocopy of the manuscript.[12] In other words, whoever deleted the copula *we-* before *shakhlel* wanted to give a clear meaning to the sentence, which had become incomprehensible due to the particle *de-* before *YYY'*—namely, it was the son of God, the Logos of the New Testament, who through the wisdom of God perfected creation.

Unfortunately, we do not know how this Christological interpretation of the first verse of Genesis should be dated. The Codex Neofiti is the only extant manuscript of this targum, and the colophon dates the manuscript to 1504. The targum itself was dated to the first century CE by its discoverer, Alejandro Díez Macho,[13] but this early dating has not found general acceptance. Today it is assumed to have been written in the fourth century.[14] But what was the original version of Genesis 1:1? The *we-* before *shakhlel* was definitely in the original manuscript text, but it is also true that the particle *de-* before *YYY'*, which makes it impossible to read *bera* as a verb and confuses the syntax of the sentence, was in the original manuscript text as well. The most probable and theologically least unsettling explanation of the extant version of Genesis 1:1 is that the clearly Christological interpretation was the work of an early modern Christian redactor.[15] On the other hand, it cannot be entirely ruled out that the reading *bera de-YYY'* (son of God) was intended in the original targum text, and that the manuscript scribe continued in the early sixteenth century with *we-shakhlel* (and perfected), because this was familiar to him from other versions of the targum (as documented in the Fragment Targum). In this case, here we would have an interpretation of the first verse of Genesis that is utterly unique in rabbinic tradition,[16] which against the background of the early Jewish evidence discussed here, however, does not seem as singular as it might appear at first glance.

3

The Divinized Human
in the Self-Glorification
Hymn from Qumran

AMONG THE MANY WRITINGS of the community that had withdrawn from Jerusalem to the Dead Sea to dedicate itself to its apocalyptic fantasies of the end of days is the so-called Self-Glorification Hymn from Qumran. The author of this enigmatic and, among scholars, disputed hymn is unknown, and only fragments of it are extant. It was written in the late Hasmonaean or early Herodian period—that is, the second half of the first century BCE. In it, an unidentified hero boasts that he was elevated among and even above the angels in heaven:[1]

(3) He established his truth of old, and the secrets of his devising (*razei 'ormato*) throughout all [generations

(4) [ ] and the council of the humble (*'asat evyonim*) for an everlasting congregation.

(5) [for]ever a mighty throne (*kisse 'oz*) in the congregation of the gods (*elim*). None of the ancient[2] kings shall sit in it, and their nobles shall not [

(6) [ ] shall not be like my glory (*kevodi*), and none shall be exalted save me, nor shall come against me. For I

have taken my seat in a/the [throne] in the heavens
(*ki ani yashavti be ... be-shamayyim*) and none [

(7) [ ] I shall be reckoned with the gods (*ani 'im elim et-hashev*), and my dwelling place is in the holy congregation (*u-mekhoni be-'adat qodesh*). [I] do not de[sire] as would a man of flesh [ ] everything precious to me is in the glory of

(8) [the gods in the] holy dwelling place (*bi-me'on ha-qodesh*). Who has been despised on my account (*mi la-vuz nehshav bi*)? And who can be compared with me in my glory (*u-mi bi-khvodi yiddameh li*)? Who [

(9) [ ] who be[ars all] griefs as I do? And who [suff]ers evil like me? No one! I was instructed and (any) teaching (*horayah*) will not be equal to my

(10) [teaching]. And who will stop me from speaking when [I] op[en my mouth]? And who shall measure the flow of my speech, and who shall be my equal, and be like (me) in my judgment?

(11) [Friend of the King (*yedid ha-melekh*), companion of holy ones (I am named)], for I shall be reckoned with the gods (*elim*), and my glory (*kevodi*) with [that of] the King's sons (*bene ha-melekh*).

This text raises many questions, not only because it is fragmentary. I will highlight only a few particularly important points here.[3] The speaker, definitely a human being, is sitting on a throne in heaven among the divine beings (the angels; in these texts, *elim* is a term denoting the angels). His glory and exaltation are unique. The elevated status of the speaker is emphasized by the fact that neither "ancient kings" nor "nobles" can sit on this throne. The kings are likely the Israelite kings of the Hebrew Bible, or more precisely the kings of the Davidic dynasty. As the speaker also feels superior in particular to them, he is evidently asserting a claim to messianic qualities.

Two parallel fragments of the hymn take the superior, angel-like status of the author yet further. There the speaker asks explicitly, "Who is like me among the divine beings?" (*mi kamoni ba-'elim*);[4] this is a rhetorical question, with which he evidently means, Who else is like me among the angels? Is there anyone else who is as elevated as I am among the angels or above them? And the answer is of course, No! The question, though, is by no means as innocent as it sounds, as it clearly alludes to Exodus 15:11, where the question refers to God: "Who is like you, O Lord, among the gods/angels?" (*mi kamokha ba-'elim YHWH*).[5] This definitely means, Is there anyone among the gods/angels, who is like you, God, who could be compared with you? And again the answer is, No! There is reason to suspect that the speaker not only boldly compares himself with the angels but also with God, even almost taking the place of God: he is not merely a particularly high angel among the angels but rather like God unique among the angels. Yet this special status bordering on hubris is only implied. When he later refers to himself as a "friend of the King" and one of many "King's sons," then he modestly steps back behind the king (God) and once again takes his place among the angels.

Another characteristic that distinguishes the speaker in his superior position is his instruction or teaching. He is the undisputed teacher, and no one can question his instruction. This suggests the reference to the Teacher of Righteousness, the outstanding leadership figure of the Qumran sect.[6] What does not at all conform with the image up to now of the uniqueness and superiority of the speaker are the statements in lines 8 and 9. Juxtaposed with the statement on glory in line 8 is the odd expression *mi la-vuz nehshav bi*, which was translated above as "Who has been despised on my account?" and literally might mean, "Who has been attributed to me, to be despised?"—that is, Who is despised and thus associated with me? The answer here too is probably, No one! The speaker is despised, and with respect to this particular contempt, no one is like him.[7] This refers directly to the suffering servant of God in Isaiah, about whom it is also said that he is "despised" (*nivzeh*), a "man of suffering," who "has borne our infirmities" (Isa. 53:3–4). It is fitting that the speaker "bears all griefs" and "suffers evil" like no one else (line 9). The author thus models himself at the same time as the suffering servant of God in Isaiah 53, thereby presumably placing himself in the messianic interpretative tradition of the Suffering Servant Songs. As a suffering Messiah, he is raised up in an unparalleled manner onto a throne in heaven, which even the Israelite kings cannot claim for themselves. We can only speculate what caused the speaker to relate the aspect of suffering on himself in a virtually paradoxical manner: in addition to the tradition of the suffering Messiah, it is possibly the hostility of his opponents who question his mission and even attempt to take his life. This could be interpreted as a further reference to the historical Teacher of Righteousness.

The question as to who this speaker could be is highly controversial. Inspired by "the dominance of Michael above all the gods" (*elim*),[8] Maurice Baillet, who first published the text as a manuscript of the War Scroll (4QM), wanted to identify the speaker with the archangel Michael.[9] From the point of view of tradition history, this interpretation is conceivable, not least if the Son of Man in Daniel is interpreted as the angel Michael—but the context actually speaks against this. Why should an angel boast of being exalted among the angels, and why should an angel say about himself that he does "not desire as would a man of flesh" (line 7)? Also, the emphasis on the teaching function of the speaker gives greater support to his having earthly rather than heavenly origins. Not least for this reason, Morton Smith considered the Teacher of Righteousness to be a more suitable candidate, but he left the question open, concluding, "Nevertheless, it is probably better to suppose that the Dead Sea group or groups produced more than one preposterous poet with an exaggerated notion of his own sanctity."[10] John Collins is more cautious, suggesting an eschatological (high) priest or teacher,[11] and I have argued in favor of "some kind of Teacher of Righteousness *redivivus*:

the founder of the sect who was imagined by his later followers as elevated into heaven and expected to return at the end of time as the priestly Messiah in order to lead the members of the community in the final battle."[12]

This still seems plausible to me, but I would like to correct one point: in my book *The Origins of Jewish Mysticism*, I strongly downplayed the aspect of apotheosis or deification, and contented myself with the well-evidenced transformation into an angel.[13] I now feel that this was too limited. Whoever the hero of the Self-Glorification Hymn is, and whatever his function at the end of days, he is a human being who in a unique manner is exalted into heaven and enthroned there. We do not hear of anything comparable regarding any other human—with the exception of Enoch, who becomes the Son of Man in the Similitudes of the Ethiopic Book of Enoch. Our hero is not just one angel among many angels, and it is not said that he will be transformed into an angel. Rather, he is and remains a human being who is elevated to the status of a god, and as such will return to earth. Certainly, "in no case does this 'divinization' impinge on the supremacy of the Most High, the God of Israel"[14] and the distance between our hero and God remains intact. And yet the divinization of a human being can hardly be driven any further. Israel Knohl therefore sees our hero not simply as another Qumran Messiah but instead as a real, direct precursor to Jesus, who then influenced Jesus and the Christian notion of the Messiah.[15]

4

The Son of God and Son of the Most High in the Daniel Apocryphon from Qumran

ANOTHER TEXT FROM Qumran that is relevant for our subject is the so-called Daniel Apocryphon. It refers directly to the Son of Man in the biblical Book of Daniel and has drawn attention from numerous scholars.[1] This is the fragment of an Aramaic scroll dating from the late Herodian period—that is, the last third of the first century BCE. Its particular significance comes from its unique, straightforward way of mentioning a "Son of God" and "Son of the Most High." Here is a translation based on the *Dead Sea Scrolls Study Edition*:[2]

Column I:

(1) [ ] settled [up]on him and he fell before the throne
(2) [k]ing forever. You are angry, ???
(3) [ ] your vision, and everything that shall come forever.
(4) [m]ighty ones, oppression will come upon the earth
(5) [ ] and great slaughter in the provinces
(6) [ ] king of Assyria [and E]gypt
(7) [ ] and he will be great (*rav*) over the earth
(8) [ ] they [will d]o, and all will serve

(9) [gr]eat (*rabba*) will he be called and he will be designated by his name.

Column II:

(1) He will be called son of God (*bera de-'el*), and they will call him son of the Most High (*bar 'elyon*). Like the sparks

(2) that you saw, so will their kingdom be; they will rule (several) year[s] over

(3) the earth and crush everything; a people will crush another people, and a province another provi[n]ce.

(4) *vacat* Until the people of God (*'am el*) arises and makes everyone rest from the sword. *vacat**

(5) His/Its³ kingdom will be an eternal kingdom, and all his/its paths in truth. He/It will jud[ge]

(6) the earth in truth and all will make peace. The sword will cease from the earth,

(7) and all the provinces will pay him/it homage. The great God (*el rabba*) (is) his/its strength,

(8) he will wage war for him/it; he will place the peoples in his/its hand and

(9) cast them all down before him/it. His/Its rule will be an eternal rule, and all the abysses

All scholars agree that column II, lines 4ff., recall Daniel 7. This pertains in particular to the "people of God" in line 4, which corresponds to the "people of the holy ones of the Most High" in Daniel 7:27 as well as to the emphasis of the kingdom as an eternal kingdom or eternal rule in lines 5 and 9, parallel to the everlasting dominion and kingdom in Daniel 7:14, 18, and 26–27. Also the promise that "and all the provinces will pay him homage" (line 7) clearly reflects the sentences "all peoples, nations, and

* *Vacat* (or *blank*) indicates that the scribe wanted an empty space at the beginning and end of this line.

languages should serve him" (Dan. 7:14), and "all dominions shall serve and obey them" (Dan. 7:27). These and other observations have brought scholars to conclude that the section following the *blank* at the beginning of line 4 describes the "eschatological period, at which time the people of God will be granted eternal dominion over the world."[4]

So far, so good. But then who is the "Son of God" and "Son of the Most High" in column II, line 1? In view of the statements in lines 4ff., it is tempting to identify him with the "one like a human being" or Son of Man in Daniel 7, or at least a royal Messiah figure[5] or eschatological savior figure such as Melchizedek, Michael, and the Prince of Light in the Qumran scrolls.[6] In the Melchizedek fragment from Qumran (11Q13), between the late second century and the mid-first century BCE, Melchizedek is the leader of the Sons of Light, who with his armies ushers in the year of grace and rule of judgment over the nations led by Belial, the Prince of Darkness. Psalm 82:1 refers to him,[7] which translates literally as, "Elohim will stand in the assembly of El; in the midst of Elohim he judges." The second Elohim is presumably to be understood as "gods" ("in the midst of the gods he judges").[8] The Melchizedek fragment thus plainly distinguishes between "Elohim," who is identified with Melchizedek, and "El," who is evidently equated with the Most High God. That "Elohim" stands for Melchizedek becomes clear at end of the fragment, where "Your God (*elohaikh*) is king" from Isaiah 52:7 also refers to Melchizedek, "Your God is [Melchizedek]."[9]

The fragment continues with a discussion of the relationship between the most high God El and Elohim-Melchizedek. Although Psalm 82:1 states that Elohim-Melchizedek holds judgment in the midst of the other gods, the judgment at the end of days is actually reserved for the Most High God El, as becomes clear from Psalm 7:8–9, which is cited immediately thereafter: "Return! El will judge the peoples."[10] The fragment determines that God is and remains the true judge, and that Melchizedek, however, once he liberates the Sons of Light from the hand of

Belial, carries out God's judgment: "But, Melchizedek will carry out the vengeance of Go[d's] (El) judgments."[11] Melchizedek is the second God (Elohim) beside the Most High God (El),[12] who acts as an agent and executive power of the Most High God. A similar picture is obtained from the War Scroll of Qumran (1QM). It is God himself who from the heavens leads the Sons of Light in war against the Sons of Darkness,[13] yet at the same time he appointed the Prince of Light[14] or the most high angel Michael to lead the Sons of Light in this final battle to the glorious victory:[15]

> He [God] sends everlasting aid to the lot of his [co]venant by the power of the majestic angel for the sway of Michael in ever-lasting lights, to illuminate with joy the covenant of Israel ..., to exalt the dominance of Michael above all the gods (*elim*), and the dominance of Israel over all flesh.

In view of these parallels, it seems appropriate to interpret the son of God or son of the Most High in the Daniel Aprocryphon as an angelic, second divine figure next to the Most High God.[16] This interpretation is supported by a surprising parallel from the New Testament. In the annunciation pericope in Luke 1:26–38, the angel Gabriel is sent by God to Mary to tell her that she will bear a son whom she should name Jesus:[17] "He will be great (*megas*), and will be called the Son of the Most High (*hyios hypsistou*)" (1:32). He will sit on David's throne and there will be no end to his kingdom (1:32–33). In response to Mary's question, how that should happen since she is not married, the angel answers, "The Holy Spirit will come upon you, and the power of the Most High (*dynamis hypsistou*) will overshadow you; therefore the child to be born will be holy (*hagion*); he will be called Son of God (*hyios theou*)" (1:35). This text sounds like a paraphrase of Daniel and the Apocryphon of Daniel. The same expressions are used as in the Daniel Apocryphon—"great" (col. I, line 9), "Son of the Most High" and "Son of God" (col. II, line 1)—and also the sonship of David and his everlasting kingdom (col. II, line 5) are mentioned. Some scholars therefore argue that Luke is directly dependent on the Daniel Apocryphon or at least that both sources are based on the same Jewish tradition.[18]

Other scholars are less impressed by these parallels, and even doubt the positive interpretation of the titles "Son of God" and "Son of the Most High" as a messianic or eschatological savior figure. In this respect, they refer to the context of the apocryphon and choose to interpret the Son of God / Son of the Most High in light of the indisputably negative tone of column I as one of the Hellenist kings, who were known for their divine ambitions.[19] Supported by Daniel 7 and Psalm 82:6, Michael Segal suggests that our hero should definitely have a negative connotation, though not as a historical Hellenist king but instead as the heavenly representative of one of the four Hellenist kingdoms in Daniel: "He is neither the human sovereign over an earthly kingdom nor a divine messianic figure"—and certainly not the Son of Man in Daniel 7.[20] Segal's strongest argument for the negative interpretation is the literary structure of the fragment, which he summarizes as follows:[21]

(a) I, 1–I, 8: Negative—time of trial and tribulation under the kings of Assyria and Egypt
(b) I, 9–II, 2:[22] ???
(c) II, 2–3: Negative—nations fighting against one another
(d) II, 4–9: Positive—eschatological sovereignty of the people of God

Segal finds it highly unlikely that the style of the fragment oscillates back and forth between the negative and positive poles—that is, at first from negative (lines I, 1–I, 8) to positive (lines I, 9–II, 1), then back to negative (lines II, 2–3), and finally back to positive (lines II, 4–9). He prefers to read the entire narrative up to line II, 3, as negative, having the positive turn not begin until line II, 4—highlighted by the *vacat* at the beginning of line II, 4[23] and the transitional preposition *'ad* (until).

There are some merits to this argument, but I do not find it truly convincing. My reluctance does not come from the objection that the positive interpretation of the Son of God or Son of the Most High in the New Testament rules out its negative interpretation in the Daniel Apocryphon, because the author of the Gospel according to Luke could hardly have used these epithets for Jesus if they had been used just a little earlier in such a negative and disparaging way to refer to a Seleucid king.[24] There are essentially two other reasons for my hesitation. First, despite all the weight of the narrative structure of the fragment, I am not convinced that the admittedly more chaotic shifts from negative to positive to negative to positive (that is, more chaotic than a simple transition from negative to positive) should be ruled out. It is well known that such apocalyptic texts are rarely as logical as we would like to see them.[25] Second and more important, it is unclear exactly how the statements on the events at the end of days in column II, lines 5ff., are to be understood. What is in fact the antecedent of the masculine third-person suffix (-eh, "his" kingdom," etc.) in these lines? In the English translation by Florentino García Martínez and Eibert J. C. Tigchelaar, which is the one Segal used,[26] the suffix is translated throughout as "his," and the text is understood such that the directly preceding "people of God" ('am el) in column II, line 4, is the antecedent of the suffix. This is by no means necessarily the case. For one thing, in the context of the fragment, the suffix in lines 5ff. can also refer back to the Son of God / Son of the Most High in line 1: the evil kingdoms will reign until the people of God rise up, and then the kingdom of the Son of God / Son of the Most High will be an eternal kingdom. Furthermore, it is striking that also in Daniel 7, malkhuteh (his kingdom) refers to both the kingdom of the Son of Man (Dan. 7:14) and the kingdom of the people of the holy ones of the Most High (7:27). Therefore, in my above translation I have offered both options—namely, the reference to the people of God as well as to the Son of God / Son of the Most High.[27]

If we now take a closer look at what is said specifically about the people of God or Son of God / Son of the Most High, these statements too can refer to both—though with one important exception: the judgment on earth in lines 5–6 cannot refer to the people of God but only to the Son of God / Son of the Most High. The judgment at the end of days is never carried out by the people of God, but always only by God himself or his messenger, the Messiah. Classic examples of this are not least the Melchizedek text discussed above and the Davidic Messiah-King in the Psalms of Solomon, who shall "purge Jerusalem from gentiles who trample her to destruction" (Ps. Sol. 17:22), "destroy the unlawful nations with the word of his mouth" (17:24), and "judge peoples and nations in the wisdom of his righteousness" (17:29).

I would therefore like to suggest that the ambiguity of the suffix *-eh* in column II, lines 5ff., is not coincidental but rather deliberate, and that the corresponding statements refer to *both* of the possible subjects, both the people of God and the Son of God / Son of the Most High. Just as the Son of Man in Daniel 7 represents the people of Israel in heaven, the Son of God / Son of the Most High in the Daniel Apocryphon is the representative of the people of God on earth. Both are given an everlasting kingdom, but the final act of salvation, the judgment, is reserved for the Son of God / Son of the Most High.[28] In light of this interpretation, the Son of God / Son of the Most High is clearly to be understood as a positive figure similar to the Son of Man, but with epithets extending far beyond the model familiar from Daniel. This figure, no longer the most high angel, but expressly a Son of God, thus gains an unprecedented proximity to God—and yet here too the distance to God is preserved, as it is ultimately the "great God" who comes to his aid, and makes the final victory of his son and his people possible.

5

The Son of Man–Enoch in the Similitudes of the Ethiopic Book of Enoch

THE NEXT PROMINENT FOCAL POINT of the Son of Man concept that originates from Daniel is in the so-called Similitudes. The Similitudes are part of the Ethiopic Book of Enoch and are dated by most scholars at around the turn of the first century BCE to the first century CE. One of its main features is the interest in a messianic redeemer figure, which here is called the "Son of Man," referring back to Daniel 7, or "the chosen one." The connection to Daniel is again unmistakable:[1]

> (1 Enoch 46:1) There I saw one who had a head of days,
>   and his head was like white wool.
> And with him was another, whose face was like the
>   appearance of a man;
> And his face was full of graciousness like one of the holy
>   angels.
> (2) And I asked the angel of peace, who went with me and
>   showed me all the hidden things, about that son of man
>   —who he was and whence he was (and) why he went
>   with the Head of Days.
> (3) And he answered me and said to me,

"This is the son of man who has righteousness, and
  righteousness dwells with him,
    and all the treasuries of what is hidden he will reveal;
  For the Lord of Spirits has chosen him, ..."

The "Head of Days" is the "Ancient of Days" or the "Ancient One"
from Daniel, and the "one with the appearance of a man" is the
"one like a human being" or "Son of Man" in Daniel.

Enoch's question as to the identity and origin of this son of
man is not directly answered; the answer comes somewhat later:

(1 Enoch 48:2) And in that hour that son of man was
  named in the presence of the Lord of Spirits,
    and his name, before the Head of Days [God].
(3) Even before the sun and the constellations [of the
  zodiac] were created,
[and] before the stars of heaven were made,
his name was named before the Lord of Spirits.
(4) He will be a staff for the righteous,
that they may lean on him and not fall;
He will be the light of the nations,
and he will be a hope for those who grieve in their hearts.
(5) All who dwell on the earth will fall down and worship
  before him,
and they will glorify and bless and sing hymns to the name
  of the Lord of Spirits.
(6) For this (reason) he was chosen and hidden in his
  [God's] presence,
before the world was created, and [he will remain] before
  him forever.

This text makes two key, almost-unheard-of statements. First, the
name of the Son of Man was "named" before God prior to the creation of the world. In plain terms this means that the Son of Man
was created before God created the world.[2] This directly brings to
mind the wisdom in Proverbs and Jesus Sirach: before any earthly

creation, the Son of Man was with God in heaven, virtually godlike. Second, even more dramatically, all human beings fall down
before him (v. 5), which apparently means that they worship him.
Evidently in order to avoid precisely this consequence, the German translation by Emil Kautzsch moves the aspect of worship
down to the second half of the verse, where it refers only to God:
all human beings fall down before the Son of Man, but they only
worship, glorify, and sing hymns to the Lord of Spirits—that is,
God. A distinction is thus made between the veneration of the
Son of Man and worship of God. The English translation is bolder
here, as we can see above, where "worship" also refers to the Son
of Man.[3]

Since the original text is no longer extant, it is difficult to come
to a conclusive judgment, but the thrust of the content more
likely suggests the bolder version: falling down and worshipping
as a statement about the Son of Man in the first half of the verse
belong together just as much as glorifying (or perhaps exalting),
blessing, and singing hymns as a statement about God in the second half of the verse.[4] It also cannot be ruled out, however, that
the boundaries are deliberately unclear and the text intentionally
keeps the worshipping of the Son of Man vague, only revealing it
in a somewhat concealed manner.

Not at all vague, but completely transparent and unambiguous
is the statement in the third parable.[5] There, the Last Judgment of
the Son of Man, judging over all creatures, including the powerful
of the earth, is described:

(1 Enoch 62:2) And the Lord of Spirits seated him [the Son
of Man] upon the throne of glory,
and the spirit of righteousness was poured upon him.
And the word of his mouth will slay all the sinners,
And all the unrighteous will perish from his presence.
(3) And there will stand up on that day all the kings and
the mighty
and the exalted and those who possess the land.

And they will see and recognize that he sits on the throne
   of his glory;
And righteousness is judged in his presence,
And no lying word is spoken in his presence. . . .
(5) And one group of them will look at the other;
and they will be terrified and will cast down their faces,
and pain will seize them when they see that Son of Man
   sitting on the throne of his glory.
(6) And the kings and the mighty and all who possess the
   land
will bless and glorify and exalt him who rules over all, who
   was hidden.
(7) For from the beginning the Son of Man was hidden,
and the most High preserved him in the presence of his
   might,
and he revealed him to the chosen. . . .
(9) And all the kings and the mighty and the exalted and
   those who rule the land will fall on their faces in his
   presence;
and they will worship and set their hope on the Son of Man,
and they will supplicate and petition for mercy from him.

Here the Son of Man is enthroned as the eschatological judge on
the "throne of his glory." Both the enthronement on the throne
of glory and carrying out of the judgment are attributes that are
otherwise reserved for God alone. He was at first hidden by God
and is not revealed until he assumes his function as judge, not
only of the chosen ones, but of all humanity. When those wield-
ing power on earth see him in all his glory and power, they will
not only praise him but also fall down before him and worship
him. The conclusion of the third parable[6] once again describes
this appearance of the enthroned eschatological judge appearing
on the throne of his glory:

(1 Enoch 69:29) And from then on there will be nothing
   that is corruptible;

for that Son of Man has appeared.
And he has sat down on the throne of his glory,
and all evil will vanish from his presence.
And the word of that Son of Man will go forth
and will prevail in the presence of the Lord of Spirits.

There can be no doubt: what we have here before us borders on a theophany, the appearance and revelation of God. The last part of verse 29, "And the word of that Son of Man will go forth and will prevail in the presence of the Lord of Spirits," sounds more like a somewhat half-hearted attempt to once again restrict the visual and thematic force of this theophany, and dutifully admonish readers or listeners not to equate this Son of Man with God. Actually, though, the author did just that.

This is followed by two more chapters (70–71) that turn everything that has been said so far upside down. Up to now, the Similitudes depict Enoch clearly as an earthly seer who receives visions in which he sees the heavenly Son of Man created before the creation of the world. Enoch and the Son of Man have nothing to do with each other—one is a divine figure and the other is a human being. In chapters 70–71, however, they are suddenly combined. In order to tone down this bold statement, many scholars assume that the two chapters are a later addition to the Similitudes.

The chapters begin with Enoch's name being taken from the people on earth during his lifetime and lifted up to God.[7] This is obviously an interpretation of the enigmatic passage in Genesis 5:21–24, where it is said of the antediluvian patriarch Enoch that he did not die a natural death but instead was taken away by God (*ki laqah oto elohim*) at the tender age of 365 years; all other antediluvian patriarchs lived much longer. Almost all interpreters of this verse understand this to mean that he was elevated into heaven. Enoch's ascent to heaven and apotheosis are then described in detail. He is lifted up to heaven, and sees all heavenly secrets and also the heavenly Temple with God's throne.[8] Up to this point, what is said is in agreement with the main part of the Similitudes and what we know from the (older) Book of the Watchers: Enoch is the visionary who has been elevated into heaven. Yet the tone then changes:

> (1 Enoch 71:9) And there came out of that house [the heavenly Temple]
> Michael and Raphael and Gabriel and Phanuel
> and many holy angels without number.
> (10) And with them [was] the Head of Days,
> and his head [was] white and pure as wool,
> and his garments were indescribable.
> (11) And I [Enoch] fell on my face,
> and all my flesh melted,
> and my spirit was transformed.
> And I cried out with a loud voice, with a spirit of power,
> and I blessed and praised and exalted [him].

Michael, Gabriel, Raphael, and Phanuel are the four highest angels who surround the divine throne, and the Head of Days is of course God, the "Ancient of Days" of Daniel. What is then described in verse 11 in nothing less than the transformation of the human Enoch into a divine being: his earthly body melts and he becomes a pure spirit, comparable to the angels. This is followed by an unexpected climax:

> (1 Enoch 71:13) And that Head of Days came with Michael and Raphael and Gabriel and Phanuel,
> and thousands and tens of thousands of angels without number.
> (14) And he [the angel Michael] came to me and greeted me with his voice and said to me,
> "You [Enoch] are that Son of Man who was born for righteousness,
> and righteousness dwells on you,
> and the righteousness of the Head of Days will not forsake you."

(15) And he said to me,

"He proclaims peace to you in the name of the age that is
to be,

for from there peace has proceeded from the creation of
the age,

and thus you will have it forever and forever and ever.

(16) And all will walk on your path since righteousness will
never forsake you;

with you will be their dwelling and with you, their lot,

and from you they will not be separated forever and
forever and ever.

(17) And thus there will be length of days with the Son of
Man,

and there will be peace for the righteous, and the path of
truth for the righteous,

in the name of the Lord of Spirits forever and ever."

God, accompanied by his four angels of the presence and all heavenly hosts, approaches the transformed Enoch in a procession, and Michael proclaims to him that he is the Son of Man, who will exercise righteousness, and with whose righteous dominion eternal peace will dawn for the people of Israel. This is a surprising twist that stands in distinct tension to the main part of the Similitudes, in which Enoch and the Son of Man are clearly separate. Viewed with earthly logic, the godlike Son of Man of the main part of the Similitudes cannot be identical to Enoch the human being, who is lifted up to heaven and must first be transformed into a heavenly spirit in order to become the Son of Man. But this is precisely what the author of chapters 70–71 wants us to believe.

Daniel Boyarin will not even consider the notion of a later addition to the Similitudes but instead sees in chapters 70–71 "the independent strand of very ancient tradition, in which the two originally separate ideas of God becoming man and a man becoming God are fused."[9] He takes up the distinction drawn by Moshe Idel between theophanic and apotheotic strands of tradition—the possibility that God reveals himself as a human being on earth (theophany) and the contrary notion of a human being who is elevated to become a God (apotheosis).[10] In the last two chapters of the Similitudes, he sees not only the first fusion of these two strands of tradition but also a direct predecessor of the New Testament message "of a God who became man, came down to earth, and returned home," and "of a man who became God and then ascended on high."[11] I can agree wholeheartedly with the second part of this interpretation. Without doubt, the redactor who added chapters 70–71 to the Similitudes was concerned with the apotheosis of Enoch, the transformation of the man Enoch into a god-like figure. His message was: the highest being alongside God is not one of his well-known angels and archangels but rather an angel who had previously been a man, and this man—as the Messiah— will bring justice and eternal peace to humanity. There is also no doubt that this Son of Man–Enoch of the Similitudes is part of the Jewish repertoire that the New Testament drew on.

But this still does not mean that the chapters 70–71 echo a "very ancient tradition"—we know absolutely nothing about the age of these chapters as compared with the main part of the Similitudes—or that it was the declared intention of the redactor to fuse the theophany of the Son of Man with the apotheosis of Enoch. It can just as well be the case that he was concerned solely with the elevation of the man Enoch, and was not aware of or was indifferent to the tension between this statement and that of the divine Son of Man. He was most certainly indifferent to the logic of modern scholars of religion. It is also definitely not the case that the Son of Man in the main part of the Similitudes becomes a human being, as implied in the first part of Boyarin's interpretation. He appears as the Son of Man because he looks like a human being, but he surely does not reveal himself as a human incarnated on earth. This is why the parallel with the New Testament overshoots the mark by far: the Son of Man–Enoch in chapters 70–71 is indeed a human being who becomes God, or rather godlike, but the Son of Man in the main part of the Similitudes is certainly not a God who became human, came down to earth, and then returned to heaven. Still, it is precisely the incarnation of God that is missing in the Similitudes. With the elevation of the man Enoch to the godlike Son of Man, the Similitudes go far—in fact very far—and they surely also help us understand the early Christology of the New Testament, but the claim that for that reason, "all of the elements of Christology are essentially in place then in the Similitudes"[12] is not justified by a sober analysis of the text. The father of that thought was instead Boyarin's exaggerated wish to anchor as many core messages of the New Testament as possible in early Judaism.

6

The Son of Man–Messiah
in the Fourth Book of Ezra

THE ESCHATOLOGICAL CONNOTATION of the Son of Man, as was already established in Daniel, comes to light with particular clarity in the pseudepigraphic (i.e., falsely attributed to a biblical author) Fourth Book of Ezra. It most probably originated after 70 CE, or more precisely around 100 CE, and is significant in our context because it obviously also refers back to the idea of the Son of Man in Daniel 7.[1] In the penultimate, sixth vision (chapter 13), the visionary sees the Son of Man coming on the clouds of heaven:[2]

> (13:2) And behold, a wind arose from the sea and stirred up all its waves. (3) And I looked, and behold, this wind made something like the figure of a man come up out of the heart of the sea. And I looked, and behold, that man flew with the clouds of heaven; and wherever he turned his face to look, everything under his gaze trembled, (4) and whenever his voice issued from his mouth, all who heard this voice melted as wax melts when it feels the fire.

The one "like the figure of a man" is undoubtedly the one "like a human being" in Daniel 7, although he does not only come with the clouds of heaven but at first comes up from the depths of the sea and then flies on the clouds of heaven. In contrast to Daniel, here he is not brought to God to receive dominion; instead, we now learn in great detail how he fights for this dominion and brings final redemption to the people of Israel. With his appearance, a multitude gathered from the four corners of the world "to make war against the man who came up out of the sea" (13:5). But he fights with unusual weapons:

> (13:9) And behold, when he saw the onrush of the approaching multitude, he neither lifted his hand nor held a spear or any weapon of war; (10) but I saw only how he sent forth from his mouth as it were a stream of fire, and from his lips a flaming breath, and from his tongue he shot forth a storm of sparks. (11) All these were mingled together, the stream of fire and the flaming breath and the great storm, and fell on the onrushing multitude which was prepared to fight, and burned them all up, so that suddenly nothing was seen of the innumerable multitude but only the dust of ashes and the smell of smoke.

Thus the multitude is destroyed and a peaceful multitude gathers around the Son of Man. As can be anticipated, it is the remnant of the people of Israel (13:13). Subsequently, God himself explains the vision to the seer Ezra:

> The man who was coming up out of the sea is "he whom the Most High has been keeping for many ages, who will himself deliver his creation; and he will direct those who are left" (13:26). When the preordained signs of the end occur, "then my son (*filius meus*) will be revealed, whom you saw as a man coming up from the sea" (13:32). Then the nations will cease fighting against each other and will gather together, desiring to conquer him. But he, "my Son," will "destroy them without effort by the law (which was symbolized by the fire)" (13:37–38). The peaceful multitude that is then gathered around the Son of Man are the lost ten tribes, "the people who remain" (13:49).

The "human" or "man" is the Son of Man—Messiah, who will destroy the sinners and heathen nations. In the lion vision that directly precedes this, he is described as "the Anointed One" (*unctus*), "whom the Most High has kept until the end of days, who will arise from the posterity of David, and will come and speak" (12:32). He is therefore explicitly also the Davidic Messiah. The war against the nations, however, is not a normal war with earthly weapons: the Messiah destroys them with the fire that comes out of his mouth, and this fire is identified as the fire of the law—that is, the Torah.[3] The law also plays an important role elsewhere in the Ezra Apocalypse. It has been correctly assumed that a deuteronomistic concept of history* stands behind this,[4] but one should not rule out early rabbinic influences. After all, we are chronologically at the transition to rabbinic Judaism.[5]

If the fire of the law that transforms the multitude into ashes goes far beyond the given framework of the early Jewish idea of the Messiah, then this applies all the more to the designation of the Messiah as the Son of God (the only direct parallel is the Daniel Apocryphon). This bold statement is often traced back to a later Christian revision that was not in the original text. Unfortunately, the Fourth Book of Ezra is extant only in translations (Latin, Syriac, Ethiopic, Arabic, Armenian, Georgian, and Sahidic), which probably go back to a Greek text that itself was likely based on a Hebrew or Aramaic original. The best-documented translation is the Latin one, which renders "son" throughout as *filius*. In one of two Arabic translations, though, it is rendered in 4 Ezra 13:32 as "my servant" and in the other as "my youth."[6] While "my servant" probably traces back to the Hebrew *'avdi*, the translation of "youth" likely comes from the Greek *pais*.[7] Elsewhere, the Messiah is expressly called "my son, the Messiah," which in Latin translation is rendered as *filius meus Jesus* (4 Ezra 7:28). Here, "Jesus" is obviously a Christian interpolation, which, however,

* One theory of biblical scholarship assumes a unified history of the biblical books of Deuteronomy, Joshua, Judges, 1 and 2 Samuel, and 1 and 2 Kings, which is denoted "deuteronomistic." The deuteronomistic concept of history emphasizes the law, centralization of the cult, and monotheism.

does not mean that "servant" and "son" are necessarily also to be understood as Christian. Both are documented in the Hebrew Bible too: the "servant" is "the servant of God" in Isaiah (42ff.), which could be viewed as the prototypical Messiah, and the "son" is an honorary title for the Davidic king, which establishes the messianic genealogy. In Psalm 2:7, God speaks to the Davidic king, "You are my son; today I have begotten you," and the expression "my son" (Hebr. *beni*) is rendered in the Septuagint as *hyios mou* and in the Vulgate as *filius meus*, the latter exactly as it appears in 4 Ezra. In the Second Book of Samuel, God entrusts the prophet Nathan with the prophecy to David: "I [God] will be a father to him [David's son Solomon], and he shall be a son (*ben*)[8] to me" (2 Sam. 7:14).

Hence there is no reason to reject the claim that divine sonship, which was originally reserved for the Davidic king, was transferred in the Fourth Book of Ezra to the Messiah. This Son of God–Messiah is certainly not an earthly figure, nor is he an angel, but instead a heavenly savior[9] who from the very beginning is hidden with God; although he acts on God's behalf, he virtually acts as God when his time has come. At one point it even says that he will judge the nations, reprove them, and then destroy them (4 Ezra 12:33); in other words, he will take on precisely the task that is actually reserved for God. Pointing in the same direction is the peaceful multitude gathered around the Son of Man–Messiah in the vision, after he destroyed the ungodly multitude: "Then many people came to him, some of whom were joyful and some sorrowful; some of them were bound, and some were bringing others as offerings" (13:13). This alludes to Isaiah 66:18–20, where God gathers "all nations and tongues": "They shall bring all your kindred from all the nations as an offering to the Lord ... to my holy mountain Jerusalem, says the Lord, just as the Israelites bring a grain offering in a clean vessel to the house of the Lord" (66:20). Rather than coming to God, the nations are now coming to the Messiah—or else the Messiah is God.[10] The title of son conferred on the Messiah thus goes far beyond the original biblical use of metaphors and is to be understood here literally. The Messiah in 4 Ezra is truly a son of God, a younger God alongside his father, the older God. The addition "Jesus" in 4 Ezra 7:28 only serves to show that this is exactly how Christian readers understood the text and therefore had no difficulty interpreting this Son of God–Messiah to be their Messiah Jesus Christ.

7

The Firstborn in the
Prayer of Joseph

ANOTHER ENIGMATIC TEXT that needs to be discussed here is the so-called Prayer of Joseph. Only fragments have survived—the most important of them (Fragment A) as a quotation from Origen's Commentary on John.[1] It is uncertain whether the original language was Aramaic or Greek, if it originated in Egypt or Palestine, and when it was written, although one possibility is the first century CE. The hero of the text is the patriarch Jacob, who is equated with Israel as an angel of God. Fragment A begins as follows:[2]

> I, Jacob, who am speaking to you, am also Israel, an angel of God and a ruling spirit (*pneuma archikon*).[3]

> Abraham and Isaac were created before any work. But I, Jacob, whom men call Jacob (but) whose (real) name is Israel, am he who[m] God called Israel, which means, a man seeing God, because I am the firstborn (*prōtogonos*) of every living thing to whom God gives life.

In the following, the angels Uriel and Jacob/Israel have a dispute over the hegemony in the celestial hierarchy, and Jacob/Israel insists that he is the highest angel: "the archangel of the power of the Lord and the chief captain (*archichiliarchos*) among the sons of God ... the first minister before the face of God."[4]

The conflict between the angel Jacob/Israel and Uriel brings to mind Enoch entering the celestial hierarchy as the highest angel Metatron, and the opposition to this from established angels in the Third Book of Enoch, but that is not all. The distinctive feature of this short fragment consists above all in the fact that the angel Jacob/Israel is not only a particularly high angel but also that he claims to be the firstborn in creation. His ancestors Abraham and Isaac are also preexistent, or more precisely they were created before the creation of the world, but Jacob/Israel, the third patriarch in the biblical genealogy, is in reality the firstborn before all creation: "a supreme preexisting spiritual being ..., which takes human form in Jacob and becomes the tribal ancestor of the people of Israel."[5] This is absolutely singular and lifts him up far above the common angel hierarchy. Jonathan Smith correctly indicates that this passage has a striking similarity to the archaic hymn of the son in the Epistle to the Colossians:

> (1:15) He [Jesus] is the image of the invisible God, the
>   firstborn (*prōtotokos*) of all creation;
> (16) for in him all things in heaven and on earth were
>   created,
> things visible and invisible,
> whether thrones or dominions or rulers or powers
> —all things have been created through him and for him.
> (17) He himself is before all things,
> and in him all things hold together.

Jacob/Israel as the firstborn of all creation refers back to Exodus 4:22: "Israel is my firstborn son" (*prōtotokos* in the Septuagint), but whereas the Exodus passage clearly refers to the people of Israel, the firstborn of creation is the highest angel in heaven (Prayer of Joseph) or Jesus (Colossians). Thus the angel Jacob/Israel moves very close to God. He is not God, but remains an angel; he is, however, the only living being with God before all creation, the sole servant before the face of God. The relationship of this highest angel to divine creation remains open in the Prayer of Joseph, while according to the Epistle to the Colossians, creation was created in and through Jesus, although that might be due to the fragmentary nature of the text. Because Jacob is also Israel and as such provides his services in heaven, it is to be expected that a concrete relationship to creation and especially Israel was established in the lost portion of the text. When looking back at the early Jewish tradition, we can observe an obvious similarity to Daniel—Israel's angel Michael as the "one like a human being" corresponds to the angel Israel as the highest heavenly authority next to God—as well as to the Son of Man in the Similitudes of the Ethiopic Enoch. The Son of Man, like the angel Israel, is a heavenly being created before the creation of the world. And if we look ahead to the further course of tradition history, it is certainly not by chance that Smith recognizes also the Prayer of Joseph to be a Jewish predecessor to New Testament Christology: "Rather than the Jews imitating Christological titles, it would appear that the Christians borrowed already existing Jewish terminology."[6]

8

The Logos according to
Philo of Alexandria

WITH THE ALEXANDRIAN PHILOSOPHER Philo (ca. 20 BCE–
ca. 50 CE), we are entering the world of Platonic, or more precisely Middle Platonic, philosophy in Jewish garb.[1] Philo's God is
absolutely transcendent. To refer to him, he uses the Platonic term
to on, "that which exists," or *ho agenētos*, "the Uncreated One."
We know *that* God exists, but we will never know *what* he is, his
essence. Nevertheless, emanating from this God are "forces" or
"powers" (*dynameis*), facets of the unknowable and unattainable
God, which through many stages embody the transcendent *to on*
and enable its transition down to our visible world. Heading these
forces are the Logos and Wisdom (*sophia*): Logos is responsible
for the emergence of the purely intelligible world of ideas (the
kosmos noētos) and Wisdom for the world perceived by our senses
(the *kosmos aisthētos*); the former is also called God's "elder and
firstborn son," and the latter, the "younger son" of God.[2]

Without going into the complex interplay of Logos and Wisdom according to Philo (the two are ontologically identical, but
they describe different aspects of God and his creative activity),[3]
I will limit myself in the following to the Logos. As God's actual
creative power, he is close to God and at the same time, as the
creator of the intelligible world of ideas, God and Logos are
identical:

Should a man desire to use words in a more simple and direct way, he would say that the world discerned only by the intellect (*ton noēton kosmon*) is nothing else than the Word of God (*theou logon*) when He was already engaged in the act of creation.[4]

When Philo attempts to describe more precisely the relationship between the unknowable and unattainable God and his Logos, he uses not philosophical but rather biblical language.[5] The Logos is

God's First-born (*prōtogonos*), the Word, who holds the eldership (*presbytatos*) among the angels, their archangel (*archangelos*) as it were, the ruler (*hyparchos*) with many names, for he is called: "the Beginning" (*archē*), and the Name of God (*onoma theou*), and His Word (*logos*), and the Man after His image (*ho kat' eikona anthrōpos*), and "he that sees" (*ho horōn*), that is Israel.[6]

Similarities with the Prayer of Joseph are immediately obvious. The Logos is the firstborn and oldest among the angels, and is identical with Israel. Yet Philo is more precise than the Prayer of Joseph with regard to the salvific function of the Logos reaching into the earthly world:

"We are all sons of one man" (Gen. 42:11). For if we have not yet become fit (enough) to be thought sons of God yet we may be sons of His invisible image (*tēs aeidous eikonos*), the most holy Word (*logou tou hierōtatou*). For the Word is the eldest-born image of God (*theou gar eikōn logos ho presbytatos*).[7]

We humans, although we cannot (yet) call ourselves "Sons of God," can indeed refer to ourselves as "Sons of the Logos," his "firstborn image," who elsewhere is even denoted as "second God":[8]

For nothing mortal can be made in the likeness of the most high One and Father of the universe but (only) in that of the second God (*deuteron theon*), who is his Logos.

God reaches into the earthly world of humanity through the Logos, the second God, his personified image and creator of the intelligible world of ideas. He does this through the human soul, which according to Philo is bound in the prison of the body and after death embarks on the journey to return to its true home, the world of ideas. Philo's Logos is thus God's creative power, which is not only responsible for the creation of the human soul but as the mediator between God and humans, also links the soul with God. For good reason, scholars have indicated the proximity of Philo's idea of the Logos to the prologue to the Gospel of John:

(1:1) In the beginning was the Word, and the Word was with God, and the Word was God.
(2) He[9] was in the beginning with God.
(3) All things came into being through him, and without him not one thing came into being.
(4) In him was life, and the life was the light of all people.

The only difference between Philo and the prologue to the Gospel of John is that in John, the Word becomes human. This is out of the question for Philo, even if some of the concepts or images that he uses for the Logos—such as the "Man after His image" or "he that sees"—seem to play with this idea. Judaism could hardly come any closer to that which would develop in Christology. It is therefore not surprising that Philo did not leave behind many traces in the comprehensive corpus of rabbinic literature, and his writings were forgotten or suppressed until into the early modern period. His actual career would be in Christianity—with such success that he was even viewed as one of the church fathers.[10]

TRANSITION

From Pre-Christian to Post-Christian Judaism

THIS ESSENTIALLY OUTLINES the binitarian ideas that developed in pre-Christian Judaism and can be viewed as the pool of ideas from which New Testament Christianity drew. Summarizing the range of the texts, it becomes apparent how many of them view the enigmatic godlike or semi-godlike figure alongside God to be an angel. This starts with the angel Michael in Daniel 7, the source of almost all further developments, and climaxes in the Qumran texts. This is hardly surprising, because the angels in Qumran are not by chance referred to as *elim*, "gods." The Prayer of Joseph is an outstanding example of this line of tradition in Greek literature. It is important to thereby keep in mind that the "angel" in the prayer is by no means an ordinary angel but rather a godly or godlike figure beside God. The angel connotation is missing in the wisdom literature, the Similitudes of the Ethiopic Book of Enoch, the Fourth Book of Ezra, and possibly also the Daniel Apocryphon. The part of wisdom literature that was influenced by the Bible also emphasizes the personal attributes of this second godlike being and its premundane creation, whereas the philosophically influenced part in the Wisdom of Solomon and especially Philo draws from the Platonic doctrine of emanation. The notion of a second godly figure is taken the furthest in the Son of God in the Daniel Apocryphon, the Son of Man in the main

65

part of the Similitudes, and the Son of God in the Fourth Book of Ezra. The contrary line of tradition of a man who is divinized is most pronounced in the human elevated among or above the angels in the Self-Glorification Hymn from Qumran and the man Enoch who is transformed into the Son of Man in chapters 70–71 of the Similitudes. The redemptive component, finally, is already laid out in the wisdom literature and is then accentuated in an eschatological sense in Daniel 7, the Self-Glorification Hymn, the Daniel Apocryphon, the Similitudes, and the Fourth Book of Ezra.

Christianity appropriated these binitarian rudiments and developed them further based on the ideas of the Son of Man and Logos. This is not a new insight, but one that needs to be asserted on two fronts. On one side are efforts by New Testament scholars to highlight the novelty of the New Testament and distance it from contemporary Judaism. They tend to downplay connections with the Apocrypha and Pseudepigrapha, and judge skeptically any attempts to view the New Testament as primarily Jewish scripture. On the other side are efforts by Jewish studies scholars who try to link the New Testament as smoothly as possible with Second Temple Judaism, aiming to dissociate it from later rabbinic Judaism. This applies in particular to the circle of scholars that has for some time been actively propagating a pre-Christian "Enochic Judaism,"[1] which revolves around the postbiblical Enoch and supposedly represents a mystically informed Judaism that was virtually free of all those exuberant legal qualities that are ostensibly so characteristic of rabbinic Judaism.

For a long time scholars of rabbinic Judaism therefore considered it an unwritten law that binitarian ideas were useless for Judaism since they had been usurped by Christians. Today, however, we know better. Recent research has shown that they continued to live on also in rabbinic Judaism, and were adopted in certain circles and harshly rejected by others (undeniably the majority). The following, second part of this book is dedicated to the continued life of binitarian ideas in rabbinic Judaism and early Jewish mysticism, and the polemics that developed against them. To that end, I again take up considerations that I developed in particular in *The Jewish Jesus*. These have recently given rise to a considerable echo and in part also harsh criticism.[2] I hope that a new attempt to treat this volatile subject will contribute to a deepened clarification. In doing this, repetitions cannot be avoided, but I have tried to keep these to a minimum. The figures highlighted here are the Son of Man from Daniel, David, and Enoch-Metatron.

PART II

Rabbinic Judaism and Early Jewish Mysticism

RABBINIC JUDAISM covers the period from the destruction of the Second Temple in the year 70 CE to the beginning of the Arab conquest of Palestine in the first half of the seventh century. It was a time of major upheaval, with the loss of sovereignty, which had already been increasingly restricted, the loss of the Temple, the ultimate transition from a Temple cult to a Torah-centered religion of the book and thus from the priests to the rabbis as the sole guardians of a life agreeable to God.

This epoch was greatly shaped by the literature of Palestinian and Babylonian Judaism, with the Mishnah and Tosefta as the first two systematic collections of binding legal norms, the Midrashim as the large-scale commentaries of almost all books of the Bible, and the Palestinian and Babylonian Talmuds as the comprehensive compendiums of scholarship in the two most significant centers of late antique Judaism. Also emerging during this period (with offshoots into the early Middle Ages) was the literature of early Jewish mysticism, the so-called Hekhalot literature, which began in Palestine and reached its pinnacle in Babylonia. In contrast to the bulk of the pertinent secondary literature, I will treat Hekhalot literature on equal terms with classical rabbinic literature.

9

The Son of Man in the Midrash

ALTHOUGH THE SON of Man in Daniel 7 plays a prominent role in the Jewish literature of the Second Temple and then also in the New Testament, it is minor in the rabbinic literature of the first half of the first millennium CE. The only rabbinic passage in which some scholars recognize the tradition of Daniel's Son of Man as the young God is in the Mekhilta, a relatively early Palestinian midrash dating from the second half of the third century CE. This is an exegesis of Exodus 20:2: "I am the Lord your God, who brought you out of the land of Egypt":[1]

"I am the Lord, your God (*YHWH elohekha*)" (Exod. 20:2). Why is (this) said?

For this reason. At the sea (of reeds) He [God] appeared (to them = Israel) as a mighty hero (*gibbor*) doing battle, as it is said: "The Lord (*YHWH*) is a man of war" (Exod. 15:3).

At Sinai (however) he appeared (to them) as an old man (*zaqen*) full of mercy, as it is said: "And they saw the God of Israel, etc. [and under his feet there (was something) like the work of sapphire brick (*livnat ha-sappir*)]" (Exod. 24:10). And of the time after they had been redeemed, what does it say? "And the like of the very heaven for clearness" (Exod. 24:10).

And (again) it says: "I watched until thrones were set in place [and an Ancient of Days took his seat]" (Dan. 7:9).

And it (also) says: "A river of fire issued and came forth from before him," etc. (Dan. 7:10).

(Scripture, therefore,) would not let the nations of the world have an excuse for saying that there are two powers (*shetei rashuyyot*), but (declares): "I am the Lord, your God" (Exod. 20:2).

I am (he who was) in Egypt and I am (he who was) at the sea.

I am (he who was) at Sinai.[2]

I am (he who was) in the past and I am (he who will be) in the future.

I am (he who is) in this world and I am (he who will be) in the world to come, as it is said: "See now that I, even I, am he, [that there is no (other) God besides me]" (Deut. 32:39).

And it says: "Even to old age I am the same"[3] (Isa. 46:4).

And it says: "Thus said the Lord (*YHWH*), the King of Israel and his redeemer, the Lord of Hosts (*YHWH tzeva'ot*): I am the first, and I am the last [and there is no God besides me]" (Isa. 44:6). And it says: "Who has wrought and done it? He that called the generations from the beginning. I, the Lord (*YHWH*), am first, and with the last I am (as well)" (Isa. 41:4).

Without again going into all the details, I would like to highlight only the most significant and controversial points of discussion. The subject of the midrash are the different manifestations of God—namely, once as a war hero and evidently young man (the latter is not said explicitly but instead can be deduced from the context), and once as an old man full of mercy. The young war hero reveals himself at the Sea of Reeds—that is, at the exodus of Israel out of Egypt—and the merciful old man reveals himself at Sinai—that is, when the Torah is presented to Israel. As is usual practice in the midrash, both statements are substantiated by Bible verses. In the first step, these are Exodus 15:3 for the young war hero and Exodus 24:10 for the merciful old man. This is largely undisputed. What is disputed, however, is precisely how the proof texts are to be understood, and in particular, why Exodus 24:10 proves that God reveals himself as old and merciful. The entire verse reads as follows: "And they saw the God of Israel. Under his feet there (was something) like the work of sapphire brick (*livnat ha-sappir*), like the very heaven for clearness." I have attempted to answer this question based on another midrash on Exodus 24:10, which is transmitted in Targum Pseudo-Jonathan:[4]

> Nadab and Abihu lifted up their eyes, and they saw the glory of the God of Israel; and in place of the footstool (*hypopodion*) of his feet which was placed beneath his throne (they saw) something like the work of sapphire stone—a memorial of the servitude with which the Egyptians had oppressed the children of Israel to serve in clay and bricks. There were women treading clay with their husbands, (and) there was a delicate young woman, who was pregnant and lost her fetus [she miscarried], and (the fetus) was crushed with the clay. Thereof (the angel) Gabriel descended, made a brick of it [the fetus], lifted it up to the highest heaven and put it as a footstool in place of the *hypopodion* of the Lord of the world.

The age of God, as I have argued, can be concluded from the fact that he uses a footstool, and his mercifulness follows from the story told in the Targum, which explains why Exodus 24:10 speaks of a sapphire *brick* under God's feet: this sapphire brick was truly a brick—namely, one of the bricks made by the Israelites in their slave labor, but a precious one, since the miscarried fetus of an Israelite woman had been baked into it. God used this sapphire brick as a footstool as a constant reminder of the servitude of Israel in Egypt. The midrash in the Mekhilta takes this up, thereby explaining also the last, particularly enigmatic part of the Exodus verse: "and the like of the very heaven for clearness." After God redeemed Israel from Egypt, the sapphire brick disappeared, and the heaven was shining again in its original clarity—that is, without an earthly object. Hence God revealed himself not only as old but also as merciful because he redeemed Israel from Egypt.

This interpretation evoked harsh criticism, in particular from Daniel Boyarin. He was irked by what he considered a far-fetched parallel from Targum Pseudo-Jonathan and indicated that footstools on thrones are not especially characteristic for the aged.[5] Regarding the former, the midrash in Targum Pseudo-Jonathan[6] is at least an interpretation of our verse, Exodus 24:10, and certainly no less plausible than the exegesis of the medieval commentator Rashi,[7] which Boyarin used to support his statement.[8] Regarding the latter, of course, also young kings could use a throne with a footstool, but this is not a resounding argument, as it did not necessarily prevent our midrash from interpreting the footstool as a sign of age. While this is admittedly no convincing proof of the age of God, as yet I know of no better one.

Adiel Schremer made a different suggestion. In his opinion, the midrash interprets the Hebrew *livnat ha-sappir* not to mean a sapphire *brick* (Hebrew *levenah*, constr. *livnat*) but instead a *white* sapphire (derived from the Hebrew *lavan*), concluding from this the white hair of God as an old man.[9] Yet there is no proof to support this. Boyarin is of the opinion that the midrash with this proof text is not about the old *God* but rather two different appearances of the divine *throne*: when Israel was enslaved in Egypt, the throne appeared as a sapphire brick and when they were redeemed, it appeared as clear and bright "as the very heaven for clearness."[10] I do not see this as significantly different from my interpretation (the midrash is in fact about the situation before and after Israel's redemption), except that I do not interpret the Exodus verse as referring to two different appearances of the throne. Instead, I presume that the sapphire brick following Israel's redemption disappeared entirely because God no longer needed the sapphire brick as a reminder.

Perhaps because Exodus 24:10 is weak as a proof text for the aged God, the editor of the Mekhilta subsequently added another proof text (Dan. 7:9) in a second step, and this one is watertight: God takes his seat on his throne expressly as an Ancient of Days (*'atiq yomin*), whose hair is furthermore described as white "like pure wool." Like most exegetes of the midrash in the Mekhilta, I interpret the quotation from Daniel 7:9 to be a second proof text for the old God. Boyarin again objected emphatically. He is bothered first by my considering Daniel 7:9 to be completely sufficient as a proof text for the old God, and that I declare the next verse, Daniel 7:10—"A river of fire issued and came forth from before him," etc.—to be "actually superfluous."[11] He informs me and his readers that it is a matter of course in a midrash proof text that not only the expressly cited portion applies but also the continuation, which—as is the case here—is often indicated by "etc." We do indeed drum this into our students in a basic midrash course. The question, however, is how far must we continue reading the proof text. I considered that the continuation in verse 10, "Thousands upon thousands served him [the Ancient One]," might refer to the age of the God-king, who has grown old and requires numerous servants, but have discarded the idea as rather unlikely. Then I drew attention to the fact that the end of the verse, "The court sat in judgment, and the books were opened," does not correspond to our midrash, which is intended to underscore God's mercy. Boyarin argues that judgment and mercy are not mutually exclusive, and on the contrary, only a judge can be merciful.[12] While that is true, the catch in this interpretation is that the judging God in Daniel 7 is anything but merciful. The following verses, Daniel 7:11–12, deal with the annihilation of the arrogant horn (i.e., the arrogant ruler) and that also all other beasts (i.e., kingdoms) will have their dominion taken away after a certain time. This truly cannot be a reference to a merciful judge, and I think this is why the midrash does not quote these verses. Boyarin also tacitly skips over Daniel 7:11–12 and simply claims that we need to continue reading to Daniel 7:13 in order to reach the core of the midrash.

This brings us to Boyarin's main contention: the core statement of the midrash is hidden in Daniel 7:13—that is, the verse that explicitly deals with the Son of Man: "I saw one like a human being, coming with the clouds of heaven." By merely starting the quotation from Daniel 7:10, our midrash actually refers to Daniel 7:13; thus for Boyarin, the proof text from Daniel is not, as I claim, a second proof text for the old God but instead a lot more: a *new midrash* on the old versus young God. In other words, it is a midrash that brings up the old dichotomy of two divine figures in heaven (Ancient One versus Son of Man), which can already be found in the Book of Daniel, and represents the actual bone of contention between the heretics and the rabbis. This needs to be underscored again: Boyarin finds the only Palestinian midrash on the Son of Man as a young God who competes with the old God in our Mekhilta passage, which nevertheless conceals this midrash in a Bible verse that is not expressly cited, as it does not want to openly bring up such a delicate subject.[13] In my view, this is a bold but also overblown exegesis that attempts to read something into the Mekhilta that is neither intended nor plausible.

For Boyarin, the Son of Man midrash in the Mekhilta, as interpreted by him, is so decisive because he wishes to see it as the urgently desired bridge between early Jewish apocalyptic texts and the Babylonian Talmud, in which the Son of Man interpretation is undisputed. Unfortunately, Boyarin did not make the effort to find additional Palestinian exegeses on Daniel 7 in order to underpin his theory. In any case, I am not aware of any such midrash, and Boyarin's bridge therefore proves to be extraordinarily unstable, if it even exists at all.

In his thorough analysis of the Mekhilta, Menahem Kister brought together all the available rabbinic and nonrabbinic parallels.[14] Perhaps the most significant passage is in a midrash in Pesiqta Rabbati,[15] which according to Kister can be traced back to the midrash on the Ten Commandments and might even have tannaitic—that is, much older—roots:[16]

> "Face to face [the Lord spoke to you at the mountain]." (Deut. 5:4)
>
> Rabbi Levi said: [God] faced them in many guises. To one he appeared standing, and to one seated; to one as a young

man, and to one as an old man. How so? At the time the Holy One, blessed be he, appeared on the Red Sea to wage war for his children and to requite the Egyptians, he faced them as a young man, since war is waged best by a young man, as it said: "The Lord is a man of war, the Lord is his name" (Exod. 15:3). And when Holy One, blessed be he, appeared on Mount Sinai to give the Torah to Israel, he faced them as an old man, for Torah is at its best when it comes from the mouth of an old man. What is the proof? The verse "With aged men is wisdom, and understanding in length of days" (Job 12:12); and therefore Daniel said: "I watched until thrones were set in place, and the Ancient of Days took his seat" (Dan. 7:9).

Rabbi Hiyya bar Abba said: If the whoreson (*bera di-zeneta*) should say to you, "They are two Gods," reply to him: I am the One of the sea, and I am the One of Sinai.

Rabbi Levi taught: At Sinai the Holy One blessed be he, appeared to them with many faces, with a threatening face, with a severe face, with an angry face, with a joyous face, with a laughing face, with a friendly face. How so? When he showed them the punishment of the wicked, he showed it to them with a threatening face, with a severe face, (and) with an angry face. And when he showed them the reward of the righteous in the time-to-come, he showed it to them with a joyous face, with a laughing face, (and) with a friendly face.

Rabbi Hiyya bar Abba taught: Should a whoreson say to you: "They are two Gods," reply to him: Scripture does not say [in Deut. 5:4]: "The Gods (*elohim*) have spoken (to you) face to face," but "The Lord (*YHWH*) has spoken with you [face to face]." (Deut. 5:4)

This Pesiqta Rabbati midrash is similar to our midrash in the Mekhilta: God appeared to Israel at the Sea of Reeds as a young warrior, and at Mount Sinai he revealed himself as an old man. The (only) proof text for the war hero is the same as in the Mekhilta (Exod. 15:3), and for the old man, as in the Mekhilta, there are

two proof texts given, which deviate slightly, however: instead of
the notoriously difficult verse Exodus 24:10 in the Mekhilta, the
Pesiqta cites the directly plausible verse Job 12:12 (catchword,
"aged"), whereas the second proof text from Daniel (7:9) is again
the same in both midrashim. It is striking that the similarly problematic continuation Daniel 7:10 is missing in the Pesiqta. Thus,
there is no foundation for reading another midrash on the old and
young God in Boyarin's sense into the Pesiqta version of the midrash. Daniel 7:9 serves solely to prove God's appearance as an old
man. There is no indication whatsoever for the integration of the
Son of Man from Daniel. Of course Boyarin could argue that
the Pesiqta version does not mean anything or even deliberately
avoids the dangerous exegesis that can only be deduced from the
Mekhilta. Yet it is also possible to take the view that this argument
definitely reads too much into the midrashim and the inverse
conclusion is more likely: that there never was a Son of Man midrash in the Mekhilta and the Pesiqta version is proof that Daniel
7:9 was readily used as a proof text for the old God, without any
hidden agenda regarding a young God.

The two interpretations by Rabbi Hiyya Bar Abba[17] explicitly
place the midrash in the context of binitarian ideas that here are
put into the mouth of Jesus as a voice for Christianity.[18] If Jesus
claims that there are two Gods—namely, God-Father and God-
Son—then the (first) appropriate answer to this is that God can
show himself in various guises (as a vengeful and merciful God, as
he did at the Sea of Reeds and Mount Sinai), but that at the same
time he is only one God and there are not, as the Christians claim,
two. The second answer takes up the common objection raised
(especially) by Christians, that the Hebrew name for God *Elohim*
is linguistically plural and that alone indicates more than one
God.[19] The classic counterargument refers to God's second name,
YHWH, which in the cited proof text Deuteronomy 5:4 is collocated with a singular verb and thus can only refer to a single
God.[20] It is striking here as well that for this clearly binitarian
interpretation, Daniel 7 is *not* consulted and hence is rejected—

either because our Pesiqta editors felt this was too dangerous, or (and I would like to support this) because Daniel 7 plays virtually no role regarding the dissemination and refutation of binitarian ideas in Palestinian Judaism. As long as the tediously reconstructed midrash in the Mekhilta remains the only "proof" for a Palestinian Son of Man midrash, I still see no reason to accept this and step onto the bridge built by Boyarin between the early Jewish and rabbinic traditions.[21]

Boyarin would like to underpin the ostensible bridging function of the Mekhilta with the argument that the traditions of pre-Christian Jewish apocalypticism, as they are preserved in the apocrypha and pseudepigrapha of the Hebrew Bible, extend far into rabbinic Judaism, and therefore also the Babylonian Talmud (Bavli) and the Hekhalot literature—that is, that "what we have in the Bavli and 3 Enoch represents the bricolage of a tradition developed out of old Jewish apocalyptic."[22] This is the auxiliary structure that Gershom Scholem already attempted to put together without much success[23] and that continues to find supporters even today,[24] although it remains rather unstable. No one would seriously want to doubt that apocalyptic trends experienced a revival in late rabbinic and especially post-Talmudic Judaism.[25] But the evidence in classic rabbinic Judaism is extraordinarily sparse—and that which can be found there is usually strongly rabbinized and thus tempered.[26] To be sure, apocalyptically hued passages can also be found in Hekhalot literature—such as the Apocalypse of David to be discussed in the next chapter—but these are late and fit into the picture of the post-Talmudic renaissance of apocalypticism.

The supposedly continuous line of tradition from early Jewish apocalypticism to the Babylonian Talmud and the Third Book of Enoch—with the Palestinian Mekhilta as the linking bracket in the middle—serves Boyarin as his main argument against the thesis I expressed earlier: that the binitarian traditions in the Talmud and the Hekhalot literature should be understood as a response to the firmly established Christianity in Babylonia.[27] In a pointed polemical formulation, he insinuates that I thereby made Metatron into a "converted Christian."[28] This is a grotesque misunderstanding. Neither do I fundamentally deny pre-Christian Jewish-binitarian traditions—I have simply not yet commented on them in detail.[29] Nor do I wish to construct an "originary difference between 'Judaism' and 'Christianity,'" and claim that the binitarian commonalities did not emerge until the end of late antiquity in the Babylonian Talmud and Hekhalot literature under the influence of Christianity.[30] In Babylonian Judaism, however, they are addressed and intensified in ways quite different from Palestinian Judaism, and this has to do with the different form of Christianity in these two Jewish centers. Whereas Christianity in Palestine was still nascent and only gradually breaking away from Judaism, Christianity in Babylonia was well established and dogmatically consolidated. Another reason is the distinct political conditions in the Roman and Byzantine Empires, where Christianity became the state religion, and those in the Sasanian Empire, where Christians were at times subjected to harsh persecution as supporters of Byzantium.

The Son of Man–Messiah David

VERY DIFFERENT from Palestinian Judaism is the situation in the Babylonian Talmud (the Bavli), the main document of Judaism from the region between the Euphrates and Tigris—a region that belonged to the Sasanian Empire and was still referred to by Jews as Babylonia. In the Bavli, we encounter a central and much-discussed interpretation of Daniel 7:9 that is put into the mouth of no one less than Rabbi Aqiva. It appears in two versions with different contextualizations, but the essence of both is identical. Here I will at first cite the version in Hagigah 14a, which takes up the subject of the Mekhilta:[1]

Babylonian Talmud

One verse says: His clothing was white as snow, and the hair of his head like pure wool (Dan. 7:9), and (elsewhere) it is written: His locks are curled and black as a raven! (Cant. 5:11)—There is no contradiction: one (verse refers to) (the court) in session, and the other (verse refers to) war. For the Master said: In (court) session none is more fitting than an old man, and in war none is more fitting than a young man.

One passage says: His *throne* was fiery flames (Dan. 7:9); and another passage says: [I watched] until *thrones* were set in place, and an Ancient of Days (*'atiq yomin*) took his seat! (Dan 7:9)—There is no contradiction: one (throne) for him [the

Ancient of Days], and one (throne) for David: For it has been taught (in a baraita): one was for him, and the other was for David—these are the words of Rabbi Aqiva.

Said Rabbi Yose the Galilean to him: Aqiva, how long will you treat the Shekhinah* as profane! Rather, one (throne) was for justice (*din*) and one (throne) was for mercy (*tzedaqah*).

Did he [Aqiva] accept this explanation from him [Yose], or did he not accept it?—Come and hear:[2] One (throne) for justice (*din*) and one (throne) for mercy (*tzedaqah*)—these are the words of Rabbi Aqiva.

Said Rabbi Eleazar ben Azariah to him: Aqiva, what have you to do with the Haggadah? Cease your talk (about the Haggadah), and turn to (the laws concerning) Nega'im and Ohalot! Rather, one (throne stands) for the throne and one (throne stands) for the footstool—a throne to sit upon and a footstool to rest his feet upon, as it is said: The heaven is my throne, and the earth is my footrest (Isa. 66:1).[3]

I have commented extensively on this sugya** elsewhere[4] and will limit myself here once again to the most important points germane to our context. Discussed are two examples of ostensibly contradictory bible verses that are reconciled in a Bavli-typical argumentation. Similar to the Mekhilta, the first example (Dan. 7:9 versus Cant. 5:11) refers to two different manifestations of God. In Daniel 7:9, God is described as an old man with white hair, and in Cant. 5:11, the anonymous lover, who according to rabbinic tradition stands for God, has curly black hair and is thus obviously a young man. The anonymous voice of the Bavli sees no contradiction here: when God is judging in court, he appears as an old man, and when he wages war for Israel, he shows himself as a young war hero. The "Master," also a typical figure in the Bavli, confirms this interpretation.

* The Shekhinah (literally "indwelling") is a rabbinic term for God.
** Sugya is the term for a complete, redacted unit in the Babylonian Talmud.

The second example refers to an apparent contradiction in the same verse, Daniel 7:9. First it is stated that "thrones" (plural) were set in place and an Ancient of Days took his seat, whereas directly following it is said that his throne (singular) consisted of fiery flames (the Bavli reverses the order in the Bible verse). Why would the one and only God need multiple thrones? The anonymous voice of the Bavli resolves this problem not by referring to two different manifestations of the same God but instead by referring back to two different figures, God and David. This explanation is confirmed not by the "Master" but by a tannaitic baraita,* that is, a tradition supposedly predating the Bavli, which on top of that is presented as an interpretation of Rabbi Aqiva.[5]

Aqiva's exegesis does not remain undisputed, however. Regarding the same baraita, Rabbi Yose the Galilean attacks his contemporary Rabbi Aqiva harshly, accusing him of profaning God by introducing a second figure (David) enthroned in heaven. According to Rabbi Yose, this is a matter of two different manifestations of one and the same God, as was also the case in the first example (Dan. 7:9 versus Cant. 5:11), and not about two different figures: in heaven, there are indeed two thrones. When God lets retributive justice prevail, he sits on the throne of justice, and when he reveals himself as a merciful God, he sits on the throne of mercy. Just as in the first instance the old judging God and the young war-waging God are one and the same, here too the punishing God and the merciful God remain one and the same God. Then we leave the level of the cited baraita and the anonymous voice of the Bavli speaks again, asking, Did Aqiva accept this explanation and take back his bold interpretation? The response comes in a different baraita: yes, Aqiva did some introspection,

---

* A baraita (pl. baraitot) is a smaller discursive unit that generally belongs to the earlier (tannaitic) period. Rabbinic Judaism is divided into two periods: that of the Tannaim (ca. 70 to ca. 230 CE) and that of the Amoraim (from ca. 230 to the redaction of the Babylonian Talmud in the sixth century CE).

and now also refers one throne to the punishing God and the other throne to the merciful God.

Yet even Aqiva's retraction is not accepted. Also on the baraita level, Rabbi Eleazar ben Azariah attacks his colleague Aqiva with almost unheard-of severity: keep your hands off the Haggadah* and stick to what you know—the laws regarding purity and impurity, that is, the Halakhah (Nega'im is about leprosy, and Ohalot deals with impurity spread by corpses). Eleazar ben Azariah will not even accept Rabbi Yose's interpretation, which Aqiva agreed to, and suggests that the plural "thrones" does not refer to two thrones but rather the divine throne and accompanying footstool. This serves to finally and radically temper Aqiva's interpretation: it is neither about two figures (God and David) enthroned in heaven, nor about two manifestations of God (punishing and merciful), but instead simply about God's throne—only one throne with the accompanying footstool, which in Daniel 7:9 is linguistically somewhat imprecisely referred to once as "throne" and once as "thrones."

That marks the end of the sugya in the Babylonian Talmud. One can assume that Rabbi Eleazar ben Azariah's exegesis is not only the pinnacle of the rejection of Rabbi Aqiva's interpretation but also an expression of the opinion of the anonymous Bavli redactor. Although the fact that the first baraita, beginning with the first dictum of Aqiva, confirms the resolution of the supposed contradiction between "throne" and "thrones" that is proposed by the anonymous voice of the Bavli—one throne for God and the other for David—the continuation of the baraita with the contradictory dictum of Rabbi Yose cannot be ignored but instead must be understood as the first correction of this rashly delivered interpretation. In the next step, the redactor of the artfully structured sugya confirms with a second baraita that Aqiva agreed to

---

* Haggadah refers to the non-law-related ethically and theologically relevant interpretations, in contrast to the Halakhah, which are interpretations based on biblical law.

Yose's opinion, in order to ultimately—again with the continuation of the cited baraita—reject this interpretation as well, and thus resolve the subject radically and thoroughly.

The danger that, from the perspective of the Bavli redactor, results from the interpretation of the plural "thrones" to mean two thrones (one for God and one for David) is palpable: there can be no doubt that here David cannot mean the earthly King David— that is, the elevation of David into heaven after his death—but rather the Davidic Messiah-King, who through the reference back to the Book of Daniel is understood here as the Son of Man in Daniel. In this context, it is not necessary to explicitly cite Daniel 7:13, since the David elevated to a second throne next to God cannot be anyone else but Daniel's Son of Man. Any other interpretation is hardly conceivable in view of the preceding tradition history of the Son of Man, with its final culmination in the New Testament: "And you will see the Son of Man seated at the right hand of the Power and coming with the clouds of heaven."[6] Aqiva's interpretation of David might even be so emphatically rejected precisely because of the Son of Man–Messiah Jesus in the New Testament. A David elevated to the Son of Man and enthroned next to God in heaven would thus be a rabbinic-Jewish continuation of the long Jewish Son of Man tradition, and possibly even an attempt to reclaim this tradition against its usurpation through Christianity.

The interpretation of the thrones in Daniel 7:9 to refer to God and the Messiah-King–Son of Man David is therefore pronounced or rather underpinned in the Bavli with a baraita in the name of Rabbi Aqiva, and then immediately rejected in this and a second baraita. The pivotal element in both baraitot is Rabbi Aqiva. This begs the question as to the age of especially the first baraita. I consider it unlikely that it is a genuinely tannaitic—that is, Palestinian—tradition going back to Aqiva.[7] The origin of the baraitot in the Bavli is often difficult to determine, and by no means are all baraitot genuine baraitot. The attribution of the baraita to Aqiva is particularly suspicious here, as the rabbinic approbation of Bar Kokhba, the leader in the Second Jewish Revolt against Rome in 132–35 CE, as the Messiah—whether historical or not—was forever linked to the name Rabbi Aqiva. Thus it is also no coincidence that Aqiva's proclamation of Bar Kokhba as the Messiah was just as emphatically rejected by his colleagues as his enthronement of the Messiah-King David in heaven.[8] There is therefore reason to believe that the Bavli redactor's rejection of the exegesis of Daniel 7:9 attributed to Aqiva was in fact an attack on circles that we do not otherwise know.

My theory is that these were circles close to the Babylonian Talmud in time and place—that is, within the cultural milieu not of Palestinian but rather Babylonian Judaism.[9] In other words, our sugya in the Bavli was not an attack on much older Palestinian traditions, much less on Rabbi Aqiva, but instead on Jewish opponents from the direct environment of the Bavli redactor. These adversaries represented the view, which from the perspective of the Bavli was definitely dangerous, if not heretical, that not only one God was residing in heaven but that in reality there were two "powers"—that is, Gods—sitting side by side on two identical thrones: God and David, the Messiah-king and Son of Man.

I am also of the opinion that these adversaries of the rabbis of the Babylonian Talmud should be sought within precisely those circles that we know from the Hekhalot literature—that is, the literature of the earliest form of Jewish mysticism.[10] It is certainly no coincidence that in the Talmudic and early post-Talmudic period, the radical idea of two divine powers, as we will later see in greater detail, is to be found almost exclusively in the Bavli and Hekhalot literature.[11]

That the Bavli, with its interpretation of Daniel 7:9, contests what it views as an expressly heretical opinion can be seen even more clearly within the context of the sugya in the parallel in Sanhedrin 38b. The context there is the familiar and much-repeated argument of the (nonspecified) heretics that God's name *Elohim* (linguistically plural), when collocated in various Bible verses with a plural verb, implies multiple Gods, or in any case at least two. The rabbis always counter this assertion with Bible verses in which *Elohim* is combined with a singular verb.[12] The Bavli summarizes the disputed verses as follows:

> R. Yohanan said: In all the Bible passages which the heretics have taken as grounds for their heresy, their refutation is found near at hand:
>
> (1) [And God (*Elohim*) said:] Let us make man in our image, [after our likeness] (Gen. 1:26).—So God (*Elohim*) created man in his own image (Gen. 1:27).
>
> (2) Come, let us go down and there confound their language (Gen. 11:7)—And the Lord came down to see the city and the tower (Gen. 11:5).
>
> (3) Because it was there that God (*Elohim*) had revealed (*niglu*)[13] himself to him (Gen. 35:7)—Unto God (*El*) who answered me in the day of my distress (Gen. 35:3).
>
> (4) For what great nation is there that had Gods (*Elohim*) so nigh unto it, as the Lord our God is [unto us] whenever we call upon him (Deut. 4:7).
>
> (5) And what one nation on the earth is like your people, Israel, to whom God (*Elohim*) went (*halekhu*)[14] to redeem for a people unto himself (2 Sam. 7:23).
>
> (6) Until thrones were set in place and an Ancient of Days took his seat.... His throne was fiery flames (Dan. 7:9).

Why were these [verbs in plural] necessary? To follow the argument of R. Yohanan, who said: The Holy One, blessed be he, does nothing without consulting his heavenly family,[15] as it is written, The sentence is by the decree of the watchers, and the verdict by the word of the Holy Ones (Dan. 4:14).[16] Now, that is satisfactory for all (the other verses cited), but how do we explain "until thrones were set in place" (Dan. 7:9)?—One (throne) was for him [God] and one for David. For it has been taught: One (throne) was for him and one for David—these are the words of Rabbi Aqiva.[17]

In the first three examples, Bible verses are juxtaposed in which God's name *Elohim* (formally plural) is collocated once with a plural verb and then with a singular one. The heretics conclude from the first verses that there are multiple Gods, or in any case at least two, whereas the rabbis attempt to use counterevidence to prove that it always concerns the one and only God. In the fourth and fifth examples, the refutation comes in the same verse: Gods who are close versus God whom we call on. God went (plural) to his people Israel in order to redeem them as his people (singular). In the final instance, the contradiction lies in the plural "thrones" versus "throne" in the singular.

Following a dictum of Rabbi Yohanan, the subsequent discussion in the Bavli explains the plural form of the verbs by asserting that God is always meant together with his heavenly court—that is, the angels. Yet as the anonymous voice of the Bavli immediately emphasizes, this clarification does not make sense for the last example in Daniel 7:9, as the following verse expressly states that the heavenly hosts stand to serve God. Although the continuation of the verse is "and the court sat in judgment," and one could conclude that this court is the heavenly hosts, who first stand attending him and then take a seat as a heavenly court, this is obviously not the compromise that the Bavli chooses to pursue; it cites the baraita of Aqiva with the following discussion, which as we have seen, culminates with "thrones" in the plural referring to the one throne with the accompanying footstool.

The context in Sanhedrin 38b thus places Daniel 7:9 into the much-discussed sequence of the disputed Bible verses. Just as in the other examples, the verb in singular makes it clear that God's name in plural does not mean two or more Gods, here the singular "throne" shows that the preceding plural "thrones" also refers only to one figure, the Ancient of Days. The clarification process initiated by Aqiva's baraita underscores this interpretation of Rabbi Yohanan (6): all attempts to read a duality of two Gods into the plural "thrones" become moot if the "thrones" are understood as a paraphrase for the one throne with its footstool. Those who succumb to the temptation to read Daniel 7:9 as supporting the doctrine of two Gods are among the same heretics who wish to interpret God's name *Elohim* as referring to more than one God.

Apocalypse of David

The only other evidence in which David assumes a similar outstanding position as in the Talmud is the so-called Apocalypse of David in the Hekhalot literature.[18] Here we are dealing with an originally independent literary unit that was later worked into the macroform Hekhalot Rabbati. The place and time of its origin are unknown. Whereas Anna Maria Schwemer advocates an extremely early dating, based on the parallels to the New Testament and the archaic-sounding Aramaic piece in the Apocalypse,[19] in my view, the Apocalypse should be shifted to the very end of the Hekhalot tradition due not least to the close relationship with the Third Book of Enoch. I first dealt comprehensively with the Apocalypse of David as an important parallel to the elevation of David in the Bavli in *The Jewish Jesus*[20] and will only highlight the most important points here, qualified in part.

The Apocalypse begins with the angel Sasangiel—presumably identical with Metatron—revealing to Rabbi Ishmael Israel's gloomy future, a series of terrible punishments that will culminate in the destruction of Jerusalem and the Temple. When Rabbi Ishmael is so dismayed at this news that he faints, he is revived by the angel Hadarniel (also identical with Metatron). Hadarniel shows Ishmael the treasury chambers of consolation for Israel, where numerous angels weave garments of redemption and crowns of life. One of these crowns—a particularly magnificent one with

the sun, moon, and twelve stars attached to it—is prepared for
David, the king of Israel. When Ishmael asks to see David, he has
the following vision:[21]

> He [Hadarniel] sat me [Ishmael] upon his lap,
> saying to me: "What do you see?"
> I[22] answered him:
> "I see seven bolts of lightning that flash[23] like one."
> He said to me: "Squeeze your eyes (tightly)
> so that you do not shudder before[24] those,
> who went forth toward David."[25]
> Immediately all the Ofannim and Serafim[26] approached,[27]
> stores of snow and stores of hail,
> clouds of glory,
> constellations and stars,
> ministering angels and the flares of the *zevul*.*
> They say:
> "For the leader, a psalm of David.
> The heavens are telling the glory of God" (Ps. 19:1).
> Then I heard a voice of great tumult
> that came from Eden saying:
> "The Lord will be king forever" (Ps. 146:10).[28]
> And behold, David, the king of Israel, came at the head.
> And I saw all the kings[29] of the house of David behind him.
> Each one (was wearing) his crown upon his head,
> but the crown of David was brighter and more distinctive[30]
>   than all (the other) crowns.
> Its splendor reaches from one end of the world to the other.
> When David ascended to the great house of learning[31]
> that is in the *raqia'*,**
> (there) was prepared for him a throne of fire
> that is forty[32] parasangs high
> and twice (as much) in length

---

* One of the seven heavens.
** The highest of the seven heavens.

and twice (as much) in width.
When David came and sat himself down upon his throne,
prepared (for him) opposite the throne of his creator,
and all the kings of the house of David sat down before
    him,
and all the kings of the house of Israel stood behind him,
David immediately recited hymns and praises
that no ear had ever heard.
When David began and said:
"The Lord will be king forever,
[your God, O Zion, for all generations, Hallelujah!"][33]
    (Ps. 146:10),
Metatron and his entire family[34] began
and said:
"Holy, holy, holy is the Lord of hosts,
the whole earth is full of his glory" (Isa. 6:3).
And the holy creatures praise and say:
"Blessed be the glory of the Lord from his place" (Ezek.
    3:12).
And the reqi'im* say:
"The Lord will be king forever" (Ps. 146:10).
And the earth says:
"The Lord was king" (Ps. 93:1),[35]
"the Lord is king" (Ps. 10:16),
"the Lord will be king forever and ever" (Exod. 15:18).
And all the kings of the house of David say:
"The Lord will be king over the entire earth" (Zech. 14:9).

To start with the most important point, I would like to propose
the thesis that here, David is the Messiah-King elevated up to
heaven who is enthroned next to God, thus fulfilling precisely the
function that the Bavli polemicizes against so strongly.[36] I con-
nect this further with the thesis that the circles that move David

* All seven heavens.

into a virtually godlike position become tangible exclusively in the Hekhalot literature—that is, early Jewish mysticism—and in the Babylonian Talmud.

The seven bolts of lightning that flash or run like one create the dramatic opening. This obviously alludes to the four creatures in Ezekiel that run to and fro, between which the lightning bolts flash (Ezek. 1:13f.), moving in perfect harmony (Ezek. 1:12). In Ezekiel's vision, they carry the throne on which a figure is sitting that looks like a human being (Ezek. 1:26)—and without any doubt, this is God. Here, however, they accompany the manifestation or rather epiphany of David, the heavenly king. All heavenly hosts and the entire company of heaven approach David and greet him with the verse Psalm 19:1, which is then confirmed by the "voice of great tumult" with the verse Psalm 146:10. Psalm 19:1 praises the glory of God, and Psalm 146:10, the opening verse of the long version of the Qedushah (*Qedushah de-Sidra*),[37] praises the kingdom of God. These classical Bible verses are therefore quite clearly addressing God, the heavenly king. Also the "voice of great tumult" refers to God, since it is the sound that arises when the four holy creatures that carry God on his throne lift themselves up and move away from Ezekiel (3:12ff.). Yet in our Apocalypse it is not God who appears, as is expected, but instead David, the king of Israel. Hence the praise of Psalms 19:1 and 146:10 can be understood not as praise of God's glory and the kingdom of God but rather as the praise of the heavenly Messiah-King David. It corresponds with this interpretation that the heading of Psalm 19:1—traditionally translated as "To the Leader. A Psalm of David"—can also be translated as "*For* the Leader. A Psalm *for* David," and that the continuation "The heavens are telling the glory of God" could refer not to God but instead to David. Accordingly, Psalm 146:10 would praise the heavenly kingdom of David rather than the kingdom of God.

This would be a bold reinterpretation of the Psalm verses and the Qedushah, which would raise David into the position of a godlike, second king in heaven. It seems to me that there is much that supports this interpretation, such as the allusions to Ezekiel, and the dramatic appearance of David with the kings from the house of Israel and David directly following the quotation of Psalm 146:10. The unprecedented boldness of this interpretation must not prevent us from giving it serious consideration.[38] In any case, it is obvious that the scribe of manuscript New York 8128, who reads the Hebrew text as meaning "who went forth toward my beloved one (*dodi*)" instead of "who went forth toward David (*dawid*),"[39] understood the text of the Apocalypse precisely in this sense, as the beloved one refers, of course, to the beloved in the Song of Songs (Canticles), who according to the traditional rabbinic interpretation stands for God. This would be a further indication that David has taken God's place. Menahem Kister correctly reminds us that this reading is not confirmed in any other manuscript,[40] although this does not automatically mean that the New York manuscript might not present reliable and even older readings.[41] The scribe of the New York manuscript, with his reading of *dodi*, without a doubt touched on a point that is implied in the narrative style of the Apocalypse.

This applies also to other elements of the Apocalypse. First of all there is David's unique crown. The crown's splendor, reaching from one end of the world to the other, is reminiscent not only of Metatron's crown,[42] but also of the dimensions of God's limbs in the Shiʿur Qomah texts in the Hekhalot literature,[43] which reach "from one end of the world to the other,[44] as well as of the splendor of the Shekhinah, which is described in the same way in the Third Book of Enoch.[45] Here, David is evidently stylized as Metatron and supplied with the attributes of a second God. He is then enthroned on a throne of fire in the highest of the seven heavens— that is, in the heavenly Temple.[46] This throne directly recalls the throne of the Ancient of Days in Daniel 7:9, which consists of fiery flames, and that David's throne is expressly prepared for him "opposite the throne of his creator" recalls Aqiva's interpretation of Daniel 7:9 in the Bavli, according to which two thrones for God and David evidently stand next to one another.[47] Also, the

size of the throne (forty or four hundred parasangs, respectively)*
is not random: in an Enoch/Metatron piece, Metatron receives
a throne "opposite/corresponding to my [God's] throne," and
this throne measures forty thousand myriads of fire parasangs.[48]
David, the king of Israel, is conflated with Metatron, God's representative, and like Metatron, assumes an almost godlike position.

The subsequent praise of God as king is the climax of the
Apocalypse in the liturgy of the Qedushah. The entire cosmos
with David at the head quotes the Bible verses that are part of the
long form of the Qedushah: David quotes Psalm 146:10; Metatron quotes Isaiah 6:3; the holy creatures quote Ezekiel 3:12; the
seven heavens quote Psalm 146:10;[49] the earth quotes Psalm 93:1
or one of the identical parallels; and the Kings of the House of
David quote Zechariah 14:9. Here, God is clearly being addressed,
and Metatron is not a second God but instead part of the heavenly hosts. Thus this heavenly praise forms a distinct counter-
weight to the prominent position of David at the beginning of the
Apocalypse. In the end, there can and must be no doubt that God
alone, and no one else, is the heavenly and earthly king. It is the
verse from Zechariah that concludes the Qedushah that makes
this crystal clear, since the continuation in the second half of the
verse reads "on that day the Lord will be one and his name one."
The purpose of Rabbi Ishmael's vision in the Apocalypse of David
is eschatological, as Ishmael sees the heavenly events as an answer
to his concerns about Israel's future. At the end of days, when the
"day of the Lord" that Zechariah foretold has come, then God
himself will redeem his people Israel and destroy the nations.

The Apocalypse of David therefore reveals an odd tension in
its message. On the one hand, it lifts up David into a virtually
godlike position in heaven—it is certainly no coincidence that
God himself appears nowhere in the Apocalypse—whereas on

* The parasang is an ancient Persian unit of distance of varying lengths. Originally perhaps roughly six kilometers, the Hekhalot literature uses it to express enor-
mous dimensions.

the other hand, it leaves no doubt that it is God who in the end will redeem his people, Israel. This tension is difficult to resolve rationally,[50] unless we consistently think the line of thought set up in the Apocalypse through to its end, and venture to conclude that the Messiah-King David and God—who at first, in the vision of Rabbi Ishmael as he looks toward heaven, are enthroned side by side in heaven—will at the end of days merge and become one: the Messiah is God and God is the Messiah. It is not least also the quotation from Zechariah that supports such an assumption, as everything that is said there about the actions of God on the "day of the Lord" can just as well be applied to the Messiah.[51] The Apocalypse of David would thus represent another striking component in the revival and further development of binitarian ideas in the Judaism of late antiquity.

Finally, I would like to mention a remarkable parallel to the Apocalypse of David in the New Testament.[52] In the Book of Revelation, which probably was written in the time of Nero or at the end of the first century CE, the visionary who has risen up to heaven sees God sitting on his throne, surrounded by twenty-four elders on twenty-four thrones and the four holy creatures (Rev. 4). The images and symbols used come largely from Ezekiel. The four creatures praise God with the Trisagion from Isaiah 6:3, followed by the worship of the twenty-four elders. Then the lamb appears, clearly signifying the crucified Jesus, which is identified with the lion of the tribe of Judah—that is, the Davidic Messiah (Rev. 5). The four living creatures and twenty-four elders fall down before the lamb, and praise it with almost the same words with which they had previously praised God. The heavenly hosts and entire cosmos join in this song of praise, and finally praise God and the lamb together. The four holy living creatures respond by saying, "Amen," and the twenty-four elders fall down and worship God and the lamb.

There is no doubt that the crucified and risen Jesus is the Davidic Messiah and Son of Man who has taken his place next to God. The presence of two divine figures in heaven has been achieved here with a clarity that still (perhaps intentionally) remains vague in the Apocalypse of David, which is why, paradoxically, the David Apocalypse more directly implies a merging of the two figures than Revelation does. Whether or not the Jewish Apocalypse of David and the Christian Revelation are in dialogue with one another can no longer be determined. Related traditions are obviously being processed, but the completely unclear dating of the Apocalypse of David doesn't permit any more concrete statements. Opposing Schwemer's early dating, I cast my vote for a late dating, concluding that the Apocalypse of David is a response to the Revelation in the New Testament.[53] While I would like to hold on to the late dating of the David Apocalypse, I will be more cautious now about claiming that it is a direct response to the New Testament, preferring instead to leave this question open. It is of course also conceivable that the two traditions developed entirely independent of one another and that there is no direct relationship between them.

Ephrem the Syrian and John Chrysostom

A brief look at the Christian literature shows that some authors interpret Daniel 7:9 similarly to the Bavli and the David Apocalypse.[54] The most impressive parallel is in the *Contra Haereses* hymns by Ephrem the Syrian (died 373). The thirty-second hymn addresses the heresy of Marcion,[55] but more specifically it is probably directed against the dispute over Arianism in the fourth century, which dealt with the relationship of God to his son. In order to illustrate this relationship, Ephrem refers to Daniel 7:9:

> 5. He draped himself in the old age of the being that does
> not age,
> in order to give instructions about his beloved Son through
> parables.
> In the form of old age he displayed his fatherhood,
> to demonstrate that he has a Son, the Son of Man,

whom Daniel saw standing before the Ancient of Days,[56]
who took the power from the mortal kings
and gave dominion to the immortal Son of the King.
6. If only one had been described as seated,
only one throne would have been there,
but instead of one throne he [Daniel] saw thrones,[57]
thereby indicating that the Ancient of Days had a throne
    companion and Son.
The thousand upon thousands whom Daniel saw,
he saw only standing before the throne;[58]
he placed one throne for the son who was being served,
and ordained standing for the ministering angels.[59]

God, Daniel's Ancient of Days, and Daniel's Son of Man are related to each other as father and son—that is, Ephrem applies precisely that which is implied by Daniel's old and young God to New Testament Christology. The power that in Daniel's vision is taken from the earthly and thus mortal kings is transferred to the eternal and immortal son of God (Jesus). Just as in the Jewish Daniel exegesis, Jesus's claim to sovereignty comes from the fact that Daniel 7:9 refers to thrones in the plural instead of one throne: that the Son of Man Jesus is therefore God's son and throne companion, sitting on a throne next to God.[60] In contrast to God and his throne companion Jesus, the angels serving God and, explicitly, also his son are not permitted to sit but instead must stand (Dan. 7:10).

John Chrysostom drew similar conclusions from the sitting of God and his son in Daniel 7:9, and the standing of the angels in Daniel 7:10, asserting that Father and Son are completely equal as regards their claim to power and their essence.[61] Kister cannot but admit that this and similar Christian exegeses are eminently theological. What else should they be, since this concerns nothing less than the unqualified divinity of the son beside the father? Yet he doggedly resists awarding the "theology" label to the discussed Jewish exegeses, claiming they are solely exegetically motivated,

aiming only to plumb the difference between standing and sitting in heaven. In particular, he seems intent on concluding from
the purely "exegetical" aim of the Jews that they had nothing to
do with the "theological" intentions of Christians and therefore,
God forbid, Jews were not in a dialogue with Christians about the
interpretation of Daniel 7:9–10, much less polemicizing against
each other. As proof of this he offers passages of Jerome and The-
odoret, whose interpretation of Daniel 7:9 differs from that of
Ephrem and Chrysostom.[62] According to Kister, Jewish and Christian exegeses proceed in parallel yet completely unrelated to each
other, pursuing their own, different interests, moving in separate
and totally different worlds. It is hard not to resort to modern
polemics here. I will be content to conclude that I prefer to view
the Christian authors as models for a dialogue between Jews and
Christians in the fourth century—a model that, furthermore,
does not undermine my interpretation of the Jewish sources but
on the contrary emphatically confirms it.

11

From the Human Enoch to the Lesser God Metatron

JUDAISM HAS A LONG TRADITION HISTORY of the antediluvian patriarch Enoch, which begins with an enigmatic passage in the Hebrew Bible, and leads via the First and Second Books of Enoch and the rabbinic exegesis of Genesis 5:21–24 ultimately to the Third Book of Enoch, where Enoch is transformed into the highest angel Metatron. Here is a summary of the main stages.[1]

The Biblical Enoch in Genesis 5

Enoch's sole appearance in the Hebrew Bible is limited to the two genealogies of the patriarchs in Genesis 4 and 5. In the second (priestly) genealogy in Genesis 5, Enoch is the sixth patriarch after Adam, of whom it is said:

(5:21) When Enoch had lived sixty-five years, he became the father of Methuselah.

(22) After the birth of Methuselah Enoch walked with God / took his path with God (*wa-yithalekh Hanokh et ha-'Elohim*) another three hundred years, and had (other) sons and daughters.

(23) Thus all the days of Enoch were three hundred sixty-five years.

(24) Enoch walked with God / took his path with God (*wa-yithalekh Hanokh et ha-'Elohim*); then he was no more (*we-'einennu*), because God took him (*ki-laqah oto Elohim*).

This short passage provoked an avalanche of interpretations. Two questions arise immediately: What is the meaning of the odd phrasing that Enoch walked with God or took his path with God? And what is the meaning of the enigmatic sentence "he was no more because God took him"? The first question is relatively easy to answer. Enoch's walk with God is to be understood not literally but rather metaphorically. Enoch did not take a stroll with God but instead obeyed God's commandments and was thus a righteous one, in contrast to the directly following generation of the flood. Hence the translation "he took his path with God" is appropriate. There is clear evidence for this interpretation in Genesis 6:9, where it is said of Noah, the ninth patriarch, "Noah was a righteous man, blameless in his generation; Noah walked with God / took his path with God." Here, Noah's "walking with God" is obviously the conclusion drawn from the fact that he was righteous and blameless.

The answer to the second question follows from the context. Whereas regarding all other antediluvian patriarchs, after mention of the absolute length of their lifetime, it is said "and he died," this unequivocal statement is missing with respect to Enoch, replaced by the phrase "and he was no more, because God took him." We can conclude from this that Enoch, at the age of 365, did not die but instead was taken by God to a different place (presumably heaven). The Septuagint, the Greek translation of the Hebrew Bible, interprets Genesis 5:24 precisely in this way:

And Enoch was well-pleasing to God (*kai euērestēsen Enoch tō theō*), and he was not found (*kai ouch ēhyrisketo*), because God transferred/translated him (*hoti metethēken auton ho theos*) (to another place).

The Extrabiblical Tradition
in the Three Books of Enoch

This approach is taken further in the noncanonical Books of Enoch. The so-called Book of the Watchers of the First (Ethiopic) Book of Enoch—one of the oldest parts, which was written in the late third or early second century BCE—depicts Enoch's rapture to heaven, and his role as mediator between God and the fallen angels of Genesis 6:[2] God sends him to the fallen angels on earth to announce to them that they will never return to heaven. This fills the gap between the list of the antediluvian patriarchs (Genesis 5) and the narrative directly following about the fall of the angels (Genesis 6's "sons of God," who had relations with the daughters of humans, thereby provoking the flood). Some scholars even believe that material that was originally biblical, but was dropped from the Book of Genesis, survived in the apocryphal Book of the Watchers of the Ethiopic Enoch.[3] The righteous Enoch, who was taken into heaven, intervenes in the fate of the corrupted angels who had fallen to earth and been condemned forever. Noah, the only other patriarch who is expressly identified as righteous, will save the no less corrupted humankind from the flood, which will destroy everything.

The Similitudes of the First Book of Enoch, written around the turn of the eras, which were discussed above, go a significant step further. Whereas the much earlier Book of the Watchers of 1 Enoch says nothing about either the condition and status of Enoch or his later fate after being "taken"—he obviously remains the human elevated to heaven, who, however, intervenes in earthly matters—Enoch in the Similitudes is explicitly transformed into an angel and learns that he is the Son of Man of Daniel 7, Israel's redeemer, who will lead his people into a time of eternal peace. In order to carry out his mission, he cannot remain a human being but must instead become an angel—without doubt a particularly high one, close to God. The Second (Slavonic) Book of Enoch, which might have been written in the first century CE, offers no significant new perspectives on this. There as well the report culminates in the physical transformation of Enoch into an angel.[4]

The climax of this development is reached in the so-called Third Book of Enoch, which has nothing in common in terms of time or location with the first two Enoch books, except for the shared interest in the patriarch Enoch. The Third Book of Enoch is likely the most recent of the writings referred to as Hekhalot literature. Its final redaction is believed by most scholars today to have taken place between 600 and 900 CE, probably in Babylonia. Supporting this view is the close relationship between the Metatron traditions in 3 Enoch (as with Hekhalot literature in general) and the Babylonian Talmud,[5] which I discuss later in greater detail. The crucial point now is that the Third Book of Enoch—in contrast to the two earlier Enoch books—takes the decisive step from Enoch's angelification to his deification, and it does so with unmatched clarity.

In order to gain a sharper picture of the distinctiveness and boldness of the Enoch-Metatron tradition in 3 Enoch, it is essential to examine the Enoch tradition of classical rabbinic Judaism at the time of nascent Christianity. Proponents of "Enochic Judaism" propagate a direct thematic link between the three books of Enoch, and either forget or ignore the large time gap between the first two books and the third book, thereby also neglecting the fact that in between comes rabbinic Judaism, with its totally different ideas and preferences. Enoch is a perfect illustration of this difference, as the rabbis assess him very differently than their predecessors in the canonical and noncanonical Jewish tradition as well as their adversaries in the "mystical" Hekhalot literature.

Enoch's Degradation by the Rabbis

The only classical rabbinic text that deals expressly with Enoch's status is in the midrash Genesis Rabbah, dated to the late third or early fourth century. There one can read in an exegesis of Genesis 5:24:[6]

And Enoch walked with God, etc. [and he was no more, for God took him] (Gen. 5:24).

(a) Rabbi Hama ben Rabbi Hoshaya said: "['and he was no more' means] that he was not inscribed in the roll (*tomos*) of the righteous but in the roll of the wicked."

Rabbi Aibu said: "Enoch was a hypocrite, acting sometimes as a righteous, sometimes as a wicked man. (Therefore) the Holy One, blessed be he, said: While he is righteous I will take him away." ...

(b) The heretics (*minim*) asked Rabbi Abbahu and said to him: "We do not find death stated of Enoch!" "How so?" inquired he. "It is said here (with regard to Enoch) that he was 'taken,' and it is said in connection with Elijah that he was 'taken,'" said they. "If you are seeking (instances of) 'taking,'" he answered, "then it is said here (with regard to Enoch) that he was 'taken,' and it is said with reference to Ezekiel, 'Behold, I take away (*loqeah*) from you the desire (of your eyes through a sudden death)'" (Ezek. 24:16). ...

(c) A matron asked Rabbi Yose: "We do not find death stated of Enoch!" Said he to her: "If (Scripture) said, 'And Enoch walked with God' (Gen. 5:24) and was silent (afterwards), I would agree with you. Since, however, it says, 'And he was no more, for (God) took him' etc. (ibid.), (it means that) he was no more in the world, 'for God took him' (ibid.)."

The situation here is completely unambiguous. First Rabbi Hama ben Rabbi Hoshaya boldly proclaims that Enoch is wicked, and Rabbi Aibu declares him a hypocrite, who sometimes acts righteously and sometimes wickedly. This is followed by a discussion of the heretics and a Roman matron with the rabbis. The heretics and the matron cannot find any biblical proof that Enoch really died, thus (correctly) concluding that he ascended to heaven. The heretics skillfully refer to the parallel case of the prophet Elijah, whose ascent to heaven is undisputed. Since the same verb is used to describe his being taken and that of Enoch (*laqah*), a consistent conclusion would be that Enoch's being taken also means that he ascended to heaven. The rabbi's response to the heretics makes it clear, however, that this verb can also be used for an earthly death—namely, as used to refer to the death of the wife of the prophet Ezekiel. The response to the matron, in contrast, is an argument using the larger biblical context taken literally. In the Bible it does not just say, "And Enoch walked with God" (which can indeed be understood, as the matron did, to mean that he was with God), but this is followed directly by "and he was no more." If this is emphasized, then it can only mean that he is dead, since it cannot be said of someone who no longer exists that he is physically with God. The conclusion of this midrash is that according to the rabbis, Enoch was anything but righteous, and he was not elevated to heaven but instead died an ordinary death.

With this harsh outcome, the rabbis questioned the entire earlier Jewish exegetic tradition. Why? Who are the heretics and who is the matron, who insist on Enoch's ascent into heaven, thus claiming only the canonical and noncanonical Jewish tradition for themselves? The designation as heretic and matron does not bring us further, since both are collective terms for all kinds of opponents to the rabbis, denoting circles of adversaries who deviate from the rabbinic norm, both within and outside rabbinic Judaism. Hence we are not yet necessarily dealing with groups whose separation from Judaism was a well-established fact. This applies in particular also to Christianity, which was becoming more firmly established at the time of this midrash (ca. 300 CE).

The Reception of Enoch in Christianity

If we take a closer look at the extensive Christian Enoch tradition, it becomes immediately clear that as a rule, this follows the pre-Christian Jewish tradition, thus contradicting the rabbinic interpretation. The most important evidence, which is a common thread running through all Christian literature, can be found in the Epistle to the Hebrews (11:5) in the New Testament:[7]

By faith Enoch was translated (*metetethē*) so that he did not experience death; and "he was not found, because God had translated (*metethēken*) him." For before his translation (*pro gar tēs metatheseōs*) he received the testimony (*memartyrētai*) that "he had pleased God."

The Epistle to the Hebrews follows the classic tradition of Enoch's translation into heaven, referring verbatim to the Septuagint,[8] but it places the ascent in a completely new context. Here, namely, Enoch appears as the second person after Abel, in a long line of Old Testament figures who distinguished themselves through their faith, and for that reason belonged to the people of God. Enoch was followed by Noah, Abraham, Isaac, Jacob, Joseph, Moses, the people of Israel, and many other biblical heroes who stood out because of their faith. And yet this faith was insufficient, since "all these, though they were commended for their faith [by God], did not receive what was promised" (Heb. 11:39), because Jesus, the "pioneer and perfecter of our faith" (12:2), had to come first and seal the promise through his death. For Enoch this means that—very much in the sense of the pre-Christian Jewish tradition—he indeed did not die but rather was taken away to heaven. This ascent, though, was only provisional as it were and could not be completed until Jesus died at the cross. Enoch's rapture in the Old Testament thereby gains a totally new dimension, and becomes dependent on the death and resurrection of Jesus.

This New Testament interpretation of the Jewish tradition of Enoch's rapture was consistently developed further by the early Christian theologians and church fathers. I will refer only to the most significant Christian testimonies before the Council of Nicaea in 325 CE—that is, precisely the time of the cited midrash from Genesis Rabbah. An examination of the sources yields the overwhelming impression that the Christian authors follow the Septuagint and the New Testament: because Enoch was well pleasing to God, he was transferred to another place, which means that there can be no doubt that he did *not* die a natural death. Clement of Rome had already seen it that way in his First Epistle to the Corinthians (9:3) in the late first century CE:

> Let us take for instance Enoch, who, being found righteous (*dikaios*) in obedience was translated (*metetethē*), and death was never known to happen to him (*kai ouch heurethē autou thanatos*).

Justin Martyr[9] and Irenaeus argue in a similar manner in the second half of the second century, as, around 200 CE, did Clement of Alexandria, who cited Clement of Rome almost verbatim.[10] Irenaeus is also familiar with the pseudepigraphic Enoch tradition.[11] Tertullian is the first church father who gives his perception of the Jewish Enoch tradition around 200 CE a definitively Christian tone. According to him, Enoch was "translated from this world" (*de hoc mundo transtulit*) and "did not yet taste death" (*necdum mortem gustavit*), although he was uncircumcised and did not yet keep the Sabbath (circumcision and observance of the Sabbath were of course not introduced in Judaism until later). Thus Enoch became a model Christian because he showed that Christians too "may, without the burden of the law of Moses, please God" (*deo posse placere*).[12] Following the Epistle to the Hebrews, Tertullian then goes a step further and emphasizes that the fact that Enoch as well as Elijah did not suffer death is merely a preliminary stage. True immortality, according to Tertullian, is dependent on resurrection,[13] and there can be resurrection only after Jesus's resurrection. From this it follows for him that Enoch and Elijah must also die before they can be resurrected:[14]

> Enoch no doubt was translated (*translatus est*), and so was Elijah; yet they did not experience death, that is, it [death] was postponed, most certainly (*dilata scilicet*): they are reserved for the suffering of death (*morituri reservantur*), that by their blood they may extinguish Antichrist.

Hence Enoch and Elijah are in a kind of intermediate stage in which they are still alive, but have not yet been resurrected. Consequently, they can intervene in the final battle against the Anti-christ. They will die in this battle, but this death will also destroy the Antichrist and bring about the final redemption of the people of God. As such, the rapture of Enoch and Elijah takes on a completely new meaning: their death is postponed so they can intervene as decisive agents in the Christian process of salvation. Almost all other Christian authors up to the Council of Nicaea accept this Christian interpretation of the tradition of Enoch's (and Elijah's) translation.

Against the background of this Christian interpretation of the Enoch myth, it can be presumed that the wrath of the rabbis of Genesis Rabbah toward Enoch is directed against Christian or, to put it more cautiously, Christianizing circles. The rabbis certainly were familiar with the unanimous Jewish tradition of Enoch's rapture, but they could not accept that this (their very own) tradition was placed in the service of a message saying that immortality and eternal life (not only of the deceased, but also of those who were spared a natural death through God's mercy) are dependent on the death and resurrection of Jesus. This message must have seemed so unbearable to them that they were even prepared to abandon their own Jewish tradition of the rapture of Enoch and degrade Enoch categorically to a mortal human. We do not know whether—and if so, to what extent—the rabbis knew the relevant Christian authors, but chronologically (prior to 325 CE), there is absolutely no reason why such an exchange could not have taken place. At least the church father Origen is known to have had contact with rabbis in Caesarea. Also, it can hardly be a coincidence that Rabbi Abbahu, one of the two rabbis mentioned in Genesis Rabbah, stands out as a participant in discussions with Christianized heretics.[15] I deliberately say "with Christianized heretics" in order to make it clear that this process of separation was by no means taking place between two already firmly established religions (Judaism versus Christianity), yet was in the gray area of (still) Jewish circles that did not want to go so far as the church fathers but nevertheless were prepared to give Enoch a prominent position in their Judaism.

As advocates of the rabbinic form of Judaism, the authors of Genesis Rabbah were able to impose their views almost completely: Enoch largely disappeared from the rabbinic literature under their control.[16] And yet this is not the end of the story. Enoch would return—if not to say, be resurrected—to Judaism with force, in the form of the highest angel Metatron. Thus we are once again at the culmination and preliminary end point of binitarian ideas in Judaism, the Third Book of Enoch.

Enoch Becomes Metatron

The transformation of Enoch into the highest angel Metatron and hence his deification takes place in several stages in the Third Book of Enoch. It is first depicted as a direct revelation of Metatron to Rabbi Ishmael, who himself was elevated to heaven in order to view God on his throne-chariot, the Merkavah. Then it is the angel Anafiel, one of the highest angels, who takes Enoch away from the eyes of his fellow humans and causes him to be brought to heaven in a chariot of fire with horses of fire.[17] The other angels can already smell from a great distance the odor of the "one born of a woman" and complain to God about his arrival, but God calms them and praises Enoch as the only human who has not worshipped idols, the "choicest of them all."[18] God chose him to serve before the throne of glory, filling him first of all with supernatural wisdom:[19]

> Then the Holy One, blessed be he,
> bestowed upon me wisdom heaped upon wisdom,
> understanding upon understanding,
> prudence upon prudence,
> knowledge upon knowledge,
> mercy upon mercy,
> Torah upon Torah,
> love upon love,
> grace upon grace,

beauty upon beauty,
humility upon humility,
might upon might,
strength upon strength,
power upon power,
splendor upon splendor,
loveliness upon loveliness,
comeliness upon comeliness;
and I was honored and adorned
with all these excellent, praiseworthy qualities
more than all the denizens of the heights.*

Then God blesses Enoch with an immeasurable wealth of blessings, enlarges him to infinite dimensions,[20] makes seventy-two wings and 365,000 eyes grow on him,[21] and enthrones him on a throne that corresponds precisely to the divine throne of glory, and which stands at the door of the seventh and highest of the heavenly palaces.**[22] Directly following this, he lets a herald go out in front of him to announce:[23]

I have appointed Metatron, my servant,
as a prince and ruler
over all the princes of my kingdom
and over all the denizens of the heights.

With that, Enoch-Metatron becomes God's representative in heaven, his vice-regent, who acts on his behalf and whom all angels have to obey:[24]

Any angel and any prince
who has anything to say in my [God's] presence
should go before him [Metatron] and speak to him.
Whatever he says to you in my name,
you must observe and do....

* These are the angels.
** The seven heavenly palaces can be understood to mean the seven heavens.

Nothing remains hidden from Metatron. Like God he knows all secrets, not only those of the angels, but also the deepest secrets of humans:[25]

> Before a man thinks in secret,
> I see (his thought);
> before he acts, I see (his act).
> There is nothing in heaven above or deep within the earth
> that is concealed from me.

Because God loves Metatron more than all humankind and all the angels in heaven, he clothes him in a majestic robe and crowns him with a kingly crown in which forty-nine refulgent stones[26] are placed, each one shining like the sun, and its brilliance illuminating the four quarters of the world. And then, after he crowned him, God calls him "the Lesser/Younger YHWH" (*YHWH ha-qatan*), giving him his own name, the Tetragrammaton:[27]

> He set it [the crown] upon my head
> and he called me the "Lesser/Younger *YWY*"[28]
> in the presence of his whole household in the height,
> as it is written:
> "My name is in him."[29] (Exod. 23:21)

Metatron is placed at almost an equal level with God; he is the second, "lesser" or "younger" God in heaven, beside the omnipotent creator God. The Bible verse quoted as proof that Metatron carries the same name as God refers to the mysterious angel of the Lord in Exodus 23:20ff.; already in the Bible it is uncertain whether this refers to an angel or in reality God himself. Yet this does not conclude the elevation of Metatron. With his finger, which he uses as a pen of flame, God writes on Metatron's crown the letters with which heaven and earth were created. This plainly means that God has revealed all the secrets of creation to him, thus making him a coruler over heaven and earth.[30]

> Out of the abundant love and great compassion
> wherewith the Holy One, blessed be he,

loved and cherished me
more than all the denizens of the heights,
he wrote with his finger,
as with a pen of flame,
upon the crown which was on my head, (the) letters by
    which heaven and earth were created; (the) letters by
    which seas and rivers were created; (the) letters by
    which mountains and hills were created; (the) letters by
    which stars and constellations,
lightning, wind, and thunder,
thunderclaps, snow, and hail,
hurricane and tempest were created;
(the) letters by which all the necessities of the world
and all the orders of creation were created.

The other angels draw from this the desired conclusion and fall
down before Metatron, in fear and trembling:[31]

They all fell (prostrate) when they saw me
and could not look at me
because of the majesty,
splendor,
beauty,
brightness,
brilliance,
and radiance
of the glorious crown which was on my head.

Only after this does Enoch-Metatron's ultimate transformation
take place:[32]

When the Holy One, blessed be he,
took me to serve the throne of glory,
the wheels of the chariot
and all the needs of the Shekhinah,
at once my flesh turned to flame,
my sinews to blazing fire,

my bones to juniper coals,
the light of my eyes to lightning flashes,
my eyeballs to fiery torches,
the hairs of my head to hot flames,
all my limbs to wings of burning fire,
and the substance of my body to blazing fire.
On my right—those who cleave flames of fire;
on my left—burning brands;
round about me swept wind, tempest, and storm;
and the roar of earthquake upon earthquake (was) before
    and behind me.

With this, Enoch's human existence is finally and completely extinguished; he is transformed into the angel Metatron. His manifestation, however, goes far beyond what we normally associate with angels, resembling more of an apotheosis. His first task is to judge all angels in heaven and assign them their appropriate place in the hierarchy of angels.[33]

At first I sat upon a great throne
at the door of the seventh palace,
and I judged all the denizens of the heights
on the authority of the Holy One, blessed be he.
I assigned greatness,
  royalty,
  rank,
  sovereignty,
  glory,
  praise,
  diadem,
  crown, and honor
to all the princes of kingdoms,*
when I sat in the heavenly court
and the princes of kingdoms stood beside me,

---

* This refers to the domains of the angels in heaven.

to my right and to my left,
by authority of the Holy One, blessed be he.

Without a doubt, this Enoch-Metatron of the Third Book of Enoch comes closer to a second divine figure next to God than any other figure in a Jewish text of antiquity or late antiquity. Only the designation as a "Lesser God" indicates a certain gradation, but if we translate the Hebrew *YHWH ha-qatan* as "Younger God," it is not all that far from the association of a God-father and God-son as is familiar in full-blown form from Christianity.

This is indisputably the culmination of the transformation and apotheosis of Enoch-Metatron in 3 Enoch. Directly following this, in the same section of text and without any recognizable break, comes an episode that turns around everything that has been said previously—the antithesis as it were to the Metatron's elevation.

Metatron and the "Heretic" Elisha ben Avuyah/Aher

But when Aher came
to behold the vision of the chariot
and set eyes upon me [Metatron],
he was afraid and trembled before me.
His soul was alarmed (to the point of) leaving him
because of his fear, dread, and terror of me,
when he saw me seated upon a throne like a king,
with ministering angels standing beside me as servants
and all the princes of kingdoms crowned with crowns
    surrounding me.
Then he [Aher] opened his mouth and said,
"There are indeed two powers (*rashuyyot*) in heaven!"
Immediately a heavenly voice came out
from the presence of the Shekhinah and said,
"Return, backsliding children (Jer. 3:22)—except for Aher!"

Then Anafiel, the Lord,
the honored, glorified, beloved, wonderful, terrible and
    dreadful Prince,
came at the command of the Holy One, blessed be he,
and struck me [Metatron] with sixty lashes of fire
and made me stand to my feet.[34]

The protagonists here are the enthroned Metatron sitting on his throne in the seventh heaven and the mortal human Aher, who sees Metatron when ascending to heaven. Aher's true name is Elisha ben Avuyah, a respected rabbi, who would become the arch heretic of rabbinic Judaism. His nickname, Aher (literally, "an other"), perhaps alludes to the heresy depicted here. A lot of ink has been (and continues to be) used writing about this episode and its parallels in the Babylonian Talmud (see below).[35] I will not go into all the details of the controversial discussion here but instead will highlight only the elements I consider significant.

It is obvious that, as worded, the episode was not composed within the framework of the Third Book of Enoch but rather that the redactor of 3 Enoch inserted it there as a preformulated literary unit in order to counter and qualify the grandiose exaltation of Metatron, as previously described. It appears in all significant manuscripts and thus cannot be dismissed as a later addition. The redactor felt compelled to dilute the description of Metatron's radiant appearance down to the status of a common angel after just having steadily augmented it right up to its breathtaking climax.[36] Aher sees Metatron enthroned in his full grandeur in the seventh heaven[37] and cannot avoid concluding that there are "two powers" in heaven, God and Metatron. The Hebrew word *rashut*, which is traditionally translated as "power/powers," signifies "rule, dominion, authority."[38] Aher believes he has identified two entities with divine authority in heaven, and not just the one and only God.

Aher's heresy as related in this episode, which has been incorporated into the Third Book of Enoch, consists in taking Metatron precisely for whom he is according to the preceding description in 3 Enoch: a second God in addition to the creator God. Because this reading by Aher, which is branded "heresy," is consistent with the general gist of 3 Enoch, we can only conclude that the factions speaking up here disagreed with this binitarian trend. We can further assume, also in light of the parallel in the Babylonian Talmud to be discussed shortly, that the factions representing the binitarian ideas were Jewish—that is, these ideas were not an import to Babylonian Judaism from the outside.[39]

It is no less a figure than God himself who—through a heavenly voice—contradicts Aher's heresy and imposes the most severe of all rabbinic penalties on him: excommunication. While the quoted Bible verse, Jeremiah 3:22, opens up the possibility of divine forgiveness to any sinner prepared to repent and return— the entire verse reads as follows: "Return, apostate sons, *I will heal your faithlessness*"—Aher is explicitly excluded from any chance of forgiveness. His sin is so great that God cannot forgive it. After that, Metatron too is punished.[40] It is not explained why, but the reason is clear: he did not contradict Aher, who held him to be a second God, and perhaps through his magnificent appearance on the throne he had even deliberately provoked or at least accepted Aher's misunderstanding. Metatron is therefore at least complicit in Aher's "heresy" and is made to stand on his feet, which means he is dethroned and degraded to a regular angel. Thus the binitarian idea of two Gods in heaven is revealed to be heresy.

Let us now look at the parallel of this episode in the Babylonian Talmud.[41] In the Bavli, it is connected to the famous Palestinian narrative of the four rabbis who ascend to heaven, presumably in order to see God on his throne.[42] The four rabbis are Ben Azzai, Ben Zoma, our Aher, and Aqiva. Only Aqiva, the eminent figure of rabbinic Judaism, comes out of this adventure unscathed. Ben Azzai dies, Ben Zoma suffers harm, and regarding Aher it is cryptically said that he "cut down the shoots." In all four cases, the fate of the respective rabbi is mentioned only by means of a Bible verse, without any further explanation. In the case of Aher it is Ecclesiastes 5:5, and the Talmud attempts to add the following explanation:[43]

> Aher cut down the shoots. Of him Scripture says: "Do not let your mouth lead you into sin [and do not say before the angel that it was an error]" (Eccles. 5:5). What does it refer to?
>
> He [Aher] saw that permission was granted to Metatron to sit[44] and write down the merits of Israel. He [Aher] said: "It is taught as a tradition that above (lema'lah) [in heaven] there is no standing[45] and no sitting, no jealousy[46] and no rivalry, no back and no weariness. Are there perhaps—God forbid!—two powers (rashuyyot) [in heaven]!?"
>
> [Thereupon] they led Metatron forth, and flogged him with sixty fiery lashes, saying to him [Metatron]: "Why did you not rise before him [Aher] when you saw him?" Permission was [then] given to him [Metatron] to strike out the merits of Aher.
>
> A heavenly voice went forth and said: "Return, backsliding children (Jer. 3:14, 22)—except for Aher."
>
> [Thereupon] he [Aher] said: "Since I have been driven forth from that [future] world, I will go forth and enjoy this world." So Aher fell into bad ways. He went forth, found a prostitute and demanded her. She said to him: "Are you not Elisha ben Avuyah?" [But] when he tore a radish out of its bed on Sabbath and gave it to her, she said: "He is another (aher)."

The agreement with the version in 3 Enoch as well as the deviations are obvious. I will limit myself here to the central points, without discussing and explaining all the details in each case. First of all, the context is different: whereas in 3 Enoch it is about the elevation of Metatron, the Bavli version revolves around the inner-rabbinic discourse about the four rabbis who went up into heaven. The main theme is not Metatron's elevation but rather the explanation of Aher's sins and heresy. This is linked to Metatron because Aher, on his journey to heaven, sees Metatron sitting.

This "sitting" is not the excessive enthronization of Metatron as in 3 Enoch but instead simply results from the fact that Metatron functions in heaven as a scribe, which means that he sits primarily as a scribe and not as an enthroned king.

Nevertheless, Aher concludes from the seated Metatron that there might be two powers in heaven, but this "insight" is expressed in a much more reserved manner than in the Third Book of Enoch. Whereas in 3 Enoch Aher wholeheartedly declares, "There are indeed two powers in heaven!" in the Bavli he is by no means certain and adds the restricting *captatio benevolentiae*, "God forbid!" Also, his "insight" in the Talmud is justified by a sentence that is phrased in a way that makes no sense in this context: "It is taught as a tradition that above (*lema'lah*) [in heaven] there is no standing and no sitting, no jealousy and no rivalry, no back and no weariness." The mention of "standing" is completely inappropriate here. Because it is corroborated in almost all manuscripts, it must be assumed that this sentence comes from a preformed text unit that was added here by the redactor, who then neglected to delete the inappropriate word "standing."[47] For this reason, I find it pointless to speculate on the meaning of individual elements of this sentence in the context of the Aher episode.[48] It is obvious that this was originally a statement not about God, but about the angels,[49] who are standing in heaven[50] but not sitting,[51] who do not experience jealousy and rivalry among one another,[52] who have no backs,[53] and who do not get weary.[54]

In contrast to 3 Enoch, in the Bavli it is not Aher who is immediately punished after his misguided "insight," but it is Metatron who is punished first. The reason for this is explicitly mentioned: Metatron should have instantly stood up when Aher entered the seventh heaven in order to make it absolutely clear that he is not a second God, but only an angel. By remaining seated, he deliberately or else carelessly misled Aher, provoking his reaction. Hence the degrading of Metatron is much more marked in the Bavli than it is in 3 Enoch—and this effect is not attenuated by the fact that Metatron is later permitted to strike Aher's merits. Here too the final verdict is proclaimed by the heavenly voice—that is, God, who thereby unequivocally exercises his prerogative as the sole authority in heaven.

The relationship between the two versions, in 3 Enoch and the Bavli, is a popular stomping ground of scholars.[55] There can be no doubt that they are both about the same episode. That they are so closely interrelated as is normally claimed, however—that one version is the template for the other, and either 3 Enoch is dependent on the Bavli or vice versa—is in my view too narrow an interpretation and thus a futile exercise in outmoded redaction criticism. Much more probable is that they both trace back to an unknown source or even several unknown sources, which they interpret in different ways.[56] Correctly, though, there is widespread agreement that the Bavli is much more reserved than 3 Enoch, attaching great importance to Metatron's degradation, as far as this is possible within the given framework, and therefore his disempowerment.[57]

The as yet most radical conclusion from the comparison was drawn by David Grossberg, who would prefer to see the Bavli version almost entirely removed from the discussion of Metatron's elevation.[58] According to Grossberg, Elisha ben Avuyah's[59] exclamation "Are there perhaps—God forbid!—two powers [in heaven]!?" is not meant as an affirmation, but on the contrary as an implicit rejection of the false impression that Metatron gave him. The true guilty party is therefore Metatron, which is why he is punished first. The subsequent permission to strike Elisha's merits is not a divine directive but instead a demand of Metatron (which is, however, satisfied—apparently by God). What Grossberg concedes as the main problem with this interpretation is the heavenly voice that follows, expressly condemning Elisha, and excluding him from any return or forgiveness. Grossberg would like to avoid this problem by referring to the famous episode in the Bavli, according to which the rabbis deny the heavenly voice any authority over their rabbinic doctrine.[60] For Grossberg this neutralizes the weight of the heavenly voice, especially since Elisha is forgiven within the course of the Bavli narrative, albeit only after his death. The actual climax of the Bavli version is in Grossberg's view the encounter with the prostitute: after Elisha attempts to start an affair with the prostitute and after he pulls a radish out of the ground on Sabbath, she is the first to identify him as "Aher"—that is, as a heretic. Hence Aher's heresy, as Grossberg concludes, is not a "failure in orthodoxy" (as it is in 3 Enoch) but rather a "failure in orthopraxy"—that is, a failure in practicing the Torah as prescribed by the rabbis, and not a failure in some theological disputes.

Grossberg takes the inner-rabbinic discourse in the Bavli more seriously than anyone before him, but he takes it to an extreme. It is certainly correct to read the Bavli version consistently within its context, and here Grossberg offers many details that have been neglected or overlooked up to now. But these too cannot be as radically freed from any connection to the elevation of Metatron as Grossberg attempts to do. To do that he has to brush them all too much against the grain. I think the most plausible explanation remains that the Third Book of Enoch and the Bavli take up an existing tradition of the elevation of Metatron and interpret them in different ways—one rabbinizing and greatly weakening his template, and the other driving it literally to unimagined heights.

Akatriel Is Metatron and God

There is yet another version of the ascent of Elisha ben Avuyah in the Hekhalot literature, this time not the Third Book of Enoch, but as an independent literary unit titled "The Mystery of Sandalfon." It is not known where or when it was written, but in its present form it can be found only in Hekhalot literature:[61]

Elisha ben Avuyah said: "When I ascended to the *pardes*[62] I beheld Akatriel *YH*, the Lord of Hosts, who sits at the entrance to the *pardes*, and 120 myriads of ministering angels surround him, as it is said: 'Thousands upon thousands served him and myriads upon myriads, etc. [stood attending him]' (Dan. 7:10). When I saw them I was alarmed and startled, regained my composure and entered before the Holy One, blessed be he."

I said before him: "Lord of the world, you wrote in your Torah: 'Behold, to the Lord, your God, belong heaven and the heavens of heavens, etc.' (Deut. 10:14). And it is written: '[The heavens are telling the glory of God,] and the firmament declares the work of his hands' (Ps. 19:2)—one alone!"

He said to me: "Elisha, my son, have you perhaps come in order to reflect upon my mysteries? Have you not heard the parable that human beings apply?"[63]

The text breaks off here, and the continuation with the parable is missing in both manuscripts. In MS Oxford, a colophon follows, and in MS New York, the scribe adds "I found no parable" and then continues with the work *Harba de-Moshe* (The Sword of Moses).

There is no doubt that this is yet another version of the narrative on Elisha ben Avuyah's ascent to heaven and his encounter with Metatron. Here, however, Elisha is not called Aher and, as we will see, also is not a heretic. Metatron is referred to here as Akatriel[64] and assumes the same function as Metatron does in 3 Enoch and in the Bavli, and consequently, his throne stands at the entrance to the seventh heaven and not at its center. Akatriel is therefore not God.[65] But he is nevertheless served by the myriads of angels from Daniel 7:10 standing around his throne. Because the Daniel verse refers to the "Ancient of Days" and thus clearly to God, other qualities of God in addition to sitting are attributed to the angel Akatriel. It is thus not surprising that in view of this presumed second God, Elisha becomes alarmed and startled. In contrast to the version in 3 Enoch and the Bavli discussed earlier, here Elisha does not draw the heretical conclusion that there are two Gods in heaven, for which he would have been punished. On the contrary, he enters the seventh heaven and, evidently at the center, steps before the throne of God, who is clearly identified as such through the epithet "the Holy One, blessed be he."

Here something unexpected happens.[66] Elisha is transformed from the protagonist of the idea of two Gods in heaven—and thus the arch heretic—into an opponent of this idea, of which he accuses none other than God himself. He does this with two Bible verses that clarify that the heavens of heavens (that is, all seven heavens) belong to *God alone* (Deut. 10:14), and for that reason, the heavens praise the glory of *God*, and the firmament— the Hebrew word for firmament (*raqiaʿ*) in the Hekhalot litera- ture is also the technical name for one of the seven heavens— announces the work of *his* hands. In other words, he accuses God of violating his own Torah by enthroning Akatriel, surrounded by his ministering angels, at the entrance to the seventh heaven, although the Torah clearly states that there can only be one God alone. According to this version the heretic is God himself. And how does God respond? He gruffly reproaches Elisha and rather haughtily lets him know that it is not Elisha's responsibility to speculate about God's mysteries.

I do not think there is any other plausible interpretation of this episode as it has been recorded here. The fact that it breaks off at this point and we do not know the continuation does nothing to change this. Menahem Kister's attempts to argue against my interpretation are unconvincing.[67] He is not willing to even con- sider the substance of my interpretation but instead simply de- clares that the absence of a continuation means, or rather must mean, that also in this version Elisha is portrayed as a heretic: "In all traditions we know of, Elisha is declared a heretic and pun- ished (as such), and it does not at all appear that this tradition [in 'The Mystery of Sandalfon'] stands contrary to all the others.... It is entirely plausible that this tradition also describes Elisha's her- esy, but the medieval scribe did not have the continuation at hand, and (that is why) it was not passed on to us."[68] It is hard to discuss such "arguments."[69]

The Babylonian Talmud too transmits a narrative about Akatriel, which again in comparison with the text from the Hekhalot literature is instructive. There the text reads:[70]

> What does he [God] pray?—Rav Zutra bar Tuvyah said in the name of Rav: "May it be my will that my mercy may suppress my anger, and that my mercy may prevail over my (other) attributes, so that I may deal with my children according to the attribute of mercy and, on their behalf, stop short of the limit of strict justice."[71]
>
> It is taught: Rabbi Ishmael ben Elisha said: "I once entered into the innermost part [of the Sanctuary]* to offer incense and saw Akatriel *YH*, the Lord of Hosts, seated upon a high and exalted throne."
>
> He said to me: "Ishmael, my son, bless me!"
>
> I replied: "May it be your will that your mercy may suppress your anger and your mercy may prevail over your (other) attributes, so that you may deal with your children according to the attribute of mercy and may, on their behalf, stop short of the limit of strict justice!
>
> And he nodded to me with his head.

The point of departure of this short text is the question of whether or not God prays. After this question is answered affirmatively comes the question about the content of God's prayer. Rav Zutra bar Tuvyah[72] answers, in the name of Rav, a well-known Babylonian Amora of the first generation:** God wishes that the attribute of mercy might always prevail in the competition of his attributes. This alludes to the fact that among the different attributes of God, especially the attributes of mercy and strict justice are in constant conflict with each other as regards his people, Israel. If God prays, this means that he prays as it were to himself—namely, that his attribute of mercy will prevail in the end.

* The Holy of Holies.
** First half of the third century CE.

This is followed by a baraita attributed to Rabbi Ishmael ben Elisha, the no less well-known second-generation Tanna of priestly descent,* who would become a hero of the Hekhalot literature. In an obviously imagined scene, Rabbi Ishmael as a high priest enters the Holy of Holies in the Temple in Jerusalem and sees Akatriel sitting there on his throne. Most probably the author is actually thinking of the heavenly sanctuary and describes Rabbi Ishmael in his later role as a journeyer to heaven. The fact that his full name is Ishmael ben *Elisha* might not be by chance, suggesting the association with *Elisha* ben Avuyah, whose ascent ended so tragically. When Akatriel asks Ishmael to praise him,[73] the rabbi or high priest miraculously repeats precisely the prayer that God himself chooses to say, and Akatriel accepts this prayer immediately.

Yet there is no danger here of Rabbi Ishmael falling victim to the same error as Elisha ben Avuyah/Aher did, because in this Bavli episode Akatriel is clearly God and not an angel with the attributes of a second God as in "The Mysteries of Sandelfon."[74] This definitely follows not only from the fact that Akatriel is referred to as "Lord of the Hosts"—an attribute that in classical rabbinic literature is used only for God[75]—but also because he is sitting on a high and exalted throne, an allusion to Isaiah 6:1: "I saw the Lord sitting on a throne, high and exalted." Furthermore, the attributes of mercy and strict justice are reserved for God alone.

Here too, therefore, as previously in the case of the ascent of Elisha ben Avuyah, the Bavli represents the strictly "orthodox" position of the one and only God, against all temptation to introduce a second God in the Jewish heaven. God addresses his prayer not to a second God beside him; instead, in his prayer he finds himself in a discourse with himself, with his qualities or attributes, which in the Kabbalah would later become powers within the Godhead. It is certainly no coincidence that the dictum of Rav Zutra in the name of Rav on God's "inner" prayer is

---

* First half of the second century CE.

operating at precisely the same level as Rabbi Yose's harsh response to Rabbi Aqiva: that the two thrones of Daniel 7:9 are intended for the two divine attributes of justice and mercy, and not for God and the Son of Man. The Bavli's intention is consistently and fundamentally to downplay the unwelcome possibility of two Gods in heaven.

The Polemics of the Talmud against Metatron

Directly following Rabbi Aqiva's interpretation of the two thrones in Daniel 7:9 as referring to God and the Messiah or Son of Man, and the enraged protest of his colleagues, there is another Metatron-critical text in the Bavli that deserves a detailed assessment:[76]

> Rabbi Nahman said: He who is as skilled in refuting the heretics (*minim*) as is Rav Idith, let him do so; but not otherwise.
>
> A certain heretic (*mina*) said (namely) to Rav Idith: "It is written, 'And to Moses he [God] said, Come up to the Lord (*YHWH*)' (Exod. 24:1). But surely it should have stated, 'Come up to me'!"
>
> "This is Metatron,"[77] he [Rav Idith] replied, "whose name is like the name of his Master, as it is written, 'For my name is in him' (Exod. 23:21)."
>
> "But if so," [the heretic retorted,] "we should worship him (too)!"
>
> "It is written (in the same passage), however," [replied Rav Idith]: " 'Do not rebel against him (*al tamer bo*)' (Exod. 23:21), [that is,] do not mistake me for him."[78]
>
> "But if so," [answered the heretic,] "why is it stated: 'He will not pardon your transgression' (Exod. 23:21)?"
>
> He [Rav Idith] answered [the heretic]: "By our troth we would not accept him [Metatron] even as a guide/messenger (*parwanqa*),[79] for it is written, 'And he [Moses] said to him [God]: If your [personal] presence goes not,[80] etc., [do not bring us up from here]' (Exod. 33:15)."

This complex text works with important implicit premises. The protagonists are Rav Idith or Idi, probably Rav Idi/th bar Abin I, a fourth-generation Babylonian Amora (ca. 350 CE), and Rav Nachman bar Yitzchak, his contemporary, as well as an anonymous heretic. The point of departure of the discussion between Rav Idith and the heretic is the verse Exodus 24:1, in which an unidentified speaker says, "And to Moses he said, 'Come up to the Lord (*YHWH*).'" Who is "he" and who is the Lord (YHWH)? One would think, as I have also added in the above translation, that "he" is God, who tells Moses—together with Aaron, Nadab, Abihu, and seventy elders—to climb onto Mount Sinai in order to approach the "Lord." If "he" is God, however, why does God say so awkwardly "Come up to the Lord" instead of "Come up to me," and why does he use the Tetragrammaton YHWH for "Lord"? The heretic addresses precisely this problem, thus obviously setting a trap for his rabbinic adversary, because—as the continued debate shows—the heretic is of the opinion that the "Lord" refers not to God but rather a second godlike figure in heaven, the angel Metatron: He [God] says to Moses, "Come up to Metatron (YHWH)."

Immediately following this text, another verse—Genesis 19:24—is discussed in the Babylonian Talmud, further elucidating the stylistic and at the same time highly charged theological problem at its root: "Then the Lord (*YHWH*) rained on Sodom and Gomorrah sulfur and fire from the Lord (*YHWH*) out of heaven."[81] This too is a discussion between a heretic and a rabbi (Rabbi Ishmael ben Yose), but the answer does not allow for a theological dispute, simply indicating that this is the linguistic style of the Bible. The strong theological repercussions, not explicitly mentioned here, result from the preceding discussion between the heretic and Rav Idith, and also from the interpretation of Genesis 19:24 by the Christian church father Justin Martyr in his dialogue with the Jew Trypho (middle of the second century CE), where Justin says that one "Lord" refers to God the father, the creator of the world, and the other "Lord" refers to the Logos,

Jesus Christ, the son of God: "He is the Lord who received commission from the Lord [who remains] in the heavens, i.e., the Maker of all things, to inflict upon Sodom and Gomorrah that which the Logos describes in these terms: 'The Lord [Logos] rained down upon Sodom and Gomorrah sulfur and fire from the Lord out of heaven [God].'"[82]

Rav Idith immediately falls for the heretic's provocation, admitting that the "Lord" (YHWH) is Metatron and even offering an explanation for it: Metatron is the angel with the same name as God—namely, YHWH. The proof text for this (Exod. 23:21) tones it down only marginally by proving "only" that God's name is contained "in" Metatron, which presumably means "in his name." With that the heretic's trap snaps shut, and he immediately retorts, if God and Metatron have the same name (that is, YHWH), and hence the two are interchangeable, then it is only logical for us also to revere Metatron, which in plain language means that we worship him as a second God. The heretic does not even need to refer explicitly to the context of the Bible verse Exodus 23:21, which the rabbi so carelessly cited—which is unmistakably about an angel whom God will send in front of Israel and Israel must obey: "Be attentive to him and listen to his voice; do not rebel against him (al tamer bo)."[83] The rabbi tries hurriedly to refute the heretic's implicit argument with a philological trick, saying that the Hebrew al tamer bo can also mean "do not mistake me [God] for him [the angel]," and for that reason must be understood as God's warning specifically not to misconstrue the Bible text in a binitarian sense. This somewhat shrewd argument is countered instantly by the heretic with the continuation of the Bible verse Exodus 23:21: if this is just about an ordinary angel, then why does it say of him, "For he will not pardon your transgression"? Forgiving sins is, after all, a prerogative of God, and so the angel Metatron spoken of here must be a second God! Somewhat cornered, the poor rabbi can offer only a rather weak defense: we (the rabbis) would not accept him (Metatron) even as a divine messenger (that is, the usual responsibility of angels), much less as a wannabe God! We want God himself to go with us and lead us out of Egypt, not one of his angels.[84]

The controversy between the heretic and the rabbi works with two premises. First, the Bible text Exodus 23:20ff. leads to the exegetic problem of differentiating between God and his angel. The text begins with a clear distinction when it states, "I [God] am going to send an angel in front of you, to guard you on the way.... Be attentive to him," and so on, but it then becomes more ambiguous: "But if you listen attentively to *his* [the angel's] voice and do all that *I* [God] say, then *I* will be an enemy to your enemies and a foe to your foes" (v. 22). It then continues in the same manner (v. 23ff.): "When *my angel* goes in front of you, and brings you to the Amorites, the Hittites, etc.... and *I* blot them out ... and *he*[85] will bless your bread and your water; and *I* will take sickness away from among you...." This is followed by numerous *I*'s, up to the disputed verse Exodus 24:1. By the time readers reach this verse they must be completely confused, ultimately no longer knowing who is speaking. And precisely this is the basis for the discussion between the heretic and the rabbi.

The second premise is the claim that Metatron's name is like the name of his Master (God), because his (God's) name (YHWH) is in him. The Tetragrammaton is obviously not contained in the name "Metatron."[86] It can therefore be assumed—correctly, in my opinion—that this claim traces back to an older tradition that is corroborated in the Apocalypse of Abraham. There the angel Iaoel/Iahoel is characterized as the one who carries within himself the power of the ineffable name, the Tetragrammaton.[87] This means that his name consists of the Tetragrammaton,[88] combined with the theophoric ending *–el*. Iaoel/Iahoel is also one of the numerous names of Metatron and thus there is some evidence that Metatron absorbed the Iaoel/Iahoel tradition, which is why he can be referred to as the angel endowed with the power of the divine name.[89]

With his exegesis of Exodus 23:21, Rav Idith opened a Pandora's box, saying exactly what the heretic wanted to hear—namely, that

Metatron is a second divine figure next to God, as the author of the Third Book of Enoch also claimed. Of course, this is neither his personal opinion nor that of his rabbinic colleagues, but he lets himself be cornered by the heretic, who consistently has the better arguments and well-nigh imposes this conclusion on him. Rav Idith obviously rejects the heretic so vehemently because the heretic's opinion was not merely a side issue that the rabbis could simply disregard. On the contrary, it was a view that had found a place in the heart of rabbinic—or more precisely, Babylonian rabbinic—Judaism.[90] The notion of two Gods in heaven was attractive and had become, in influential rabbinic circles, even acceptable. This is the only way to explain the rabbi's harsh and yet awkward reply. There is reason to assume that here too the direct opponents of the rabbi can be found among those circles that stand behind the Hekhalot literature and especially the Third Book of Enoch.

Kister must be credited in this context for having referred to two texts among the Hekhalot literature that I edited long ago, but whose relevance for our subject here I had not recognized up to now.[91] The first text is a Metatron fragment that was previously unknown, followed by a Shi'ur Qomah piece and a description of the heavenly court. I have translated the portion that is relevant for our context:[92]

> The earth shines from his* glory, and the sun, moon, and stars glow from his light and shine. God appointed this angel as lord over all creation and made him the ruler over the forces above and below,** to guide them and lead them in their devotion.[93] All [angels] praise, sanctify, and worship [God] and say: "Holy, holy, holy [is the Lord of hosts]" (Isa. 6:3) and "Praised be the glory of the Lord from its place" (Ezek. 3:12). And this angel praises [God] together with them. He is [the angel] that God

---

* Of the angel named in the following.
** Angels and human beings.

appointed over Israel and [with reference to this] he said to Moses: "I am going to send an angel in front of you," etc. (Exod. 23:20). "Be attentive to him[94] and listen to his voice; do not rebel against him," etc. (Exod. 23:21). "But if you listen attentively to his voice and do all that I say, [then I will be an enemy to your enemies and a foe to your foes]" (Exod. 23:22).[95]

He named the name of the angel after the name of his creator, as it is said, "For my name is in him" (Exod. 23:21). He declared his [the angel's] authority (rashut) like his [God's] authority, and his [the angel's] command is deemed a command. And everyone who believes that Rabbi Ishmael intended this is wicked and a heretic,[96] and has no part in the future world. And it is proof of our words that he [God] gave him [the angel] (the) authority to issue a decree that the Holy One, blessed be he, carries out, because the Bible verse says "But if you listen attentively to his voice and do all that I say," etc. (Exod. 23:22), and not "all that he says"—from this we learn that he [the angel] issues a decree, and his creator carries it out!

It is not known where or when this was written. Again, we can only say that it is related to the Hekhalot literature. At most it is interesting that the manuscript might have come from the Iraq region—that is, belonging to the cultural sphere of Babylonian Judaism.[97] Its content, however, takes your breath away.[98] An unnamed angel is appointed the omnipotent ruler over heaven and earth, precisely in the style of Metatron in 3 Enoch. For this reason, and because directly following the translated passage Metatron is called the Angel of the Presence, there can hardly be any doubt that Metatron is the protagonist of our text. After this virtually unsurpassable elevation of Metatron, though, the mood changes: all angels in heaven praise God with the Qedushah, the Trisagion, and Metatron is one of them; in his relationship to God, he is like any other angel.

But the story does not end there. Metatron is the angel of Exodus 23:20ff., whom Israel is to obey and who carries the name of

God (obviously the Tetragrammaton YHWH), just as in 3 Enoch
and the Bavli. And now Metatron's bold elevation is repeated: God
gives him the same authority as his own; his command is God's
command. Once again the verse Exodus 23:22 serves as a proof
text, in that the verse's inherent tension between the angel and
God ("if you [Israel] listen attentively to *his* [the angel's] voice
and do all that *I* [God] say") is explicitly thematized: what God
says are actually the words of the angel, who utters them and that
are then carried out by God. The identities of God and the angel
are blurred; they remain two separate figures, but get so close to
each other that it is difficult to distinguish one from the other, as
is already laid out in the Bible verse. In view of the final sentence,
one even gets the impression that God with his authority subor-
dinates himself to the authority of the angel.

This is the most extreme statement thus far on the dominion
and authority of two Gods in heaven. For this reason it does not
come as a surprise that the unknown author of this unprecedented move contradicts himself already in the course of his text,
as did the redactor of the Third Book of Enoch by having the elevation of Metatron be followed by his degradation in the episode
on Elisha ben Avuyah/Aher's journey to heaven, asserting that
whoever attributes such a view to Rabbi Ishmael is a heretic. Of
course it is no coincidence that it is precisely Rabbi Ishmael who
is to be protected from any accusation of heresy, as next to Rabbi
Aqiva he is the most significant protagonist of Hekhalot literature. He is also the one who learns everything about Enoch-
Metatron on his journey to heaven in the Third Book of Enoch.
The fragment from the Cairo Geniza also reflects circles in which
binitarian ideas were developed and openly advocated, and here
too, as in 3 Enoch and the Bavli, we are dealing with circles within
Babylonian rabbinic Judaism that are contradicted with varying
degrees of vehemence. Yet the contradiction and polemics cannot belie the fact that the opposed "heresy" is to be found at the
heart of rabbinic Judaism; that is the only explanation for the severity of the polemics.

Also the second Geniza text from the realm of the Hekhalot literature discusses Bible verses that allow a reading involving the idea of two powers in heaven:[99]

Then came the *Ruah Pisqon*, standing between them, and all the angelic princes trembled before him. He said to him [Moses]:

Moses, Moses, I am the one who revealed himself to you on that day when your creator spoke to you, as it is said: "There the angel of the Lord, etc. [appeared to him in a flame of fire out of a bush]" (Exod. 3:2).

And I am the one who said to you: "Remove the sandals from your feet," etc. (Exod. 3:5).

And I am *Sanegoron, Pisqon, Itmon....*[100]

From here[101] said Rabbi Yehoshua:

This is the [angel], of whom Scripture says: "See, my angel shall go in front of you,"[102] etc. (Exod. 32:34), "And the Lord (*YHWH*)[103] said to Satan, [the Lord (*YHWH*) rebukes you, O Satan!]" (Zech. 3:2).

And this is the [angel], of whom Scripture says: "Then the Lord (*YHWH*) rained [sulfur and fire on Sodom and Gomorrah], etc. [from the Lord (*YHWH*)]" (Gen. 19:24).

Are there perhaps two powers (*rashuyyot*) in heaven?! [No,] but this is the [angel],[104] whose name is in the name of the Holy One, blessed be he.

The cited text is part of an extensive and relatively old Geniza fragment about a revelation to Moses in the style of the Hekhalot literature.[105] The *Ruah Pisqon*,[106] who is abruptly introduced here, is once again very likely Metatron. In any case, this name as well as the names *Sanegoron, Pisqon,* and *Itmon* a few lines further down are also attested in the Hekhalot literature as names of Metatron.[107] As in 3 Enoch, here he stands at the top of the celestial hierarchy; all angelic princes are subordinate to him. He reveals himself to Moses as the biblical angel of the Lord, and this identification is then documented by means of various Bible verses.

The first two proof texts refer to the revelation to Moses in the burning bush. Similar to Exodus 23:20ff., this is yet another text in which the fine line between God and his angel is blurred or intentionally kept vague. The initial statement that God (*Elohim*) heard his people Israel groaning and crying out in Egypt (Exod. 2:24) is followed by the revelation to Moses (Exod. 3:1ff.). At Horeb, God's mountain, the "angel of the Lord" (*mal'akh YHWH*) appears to Moses in a flame of fire out of a bush. This is the cited verse, Exodus 3:2. When God (*YHWH*) sees Moses approach the bush, God (*Elohim*) calls to him out of the bush (v. 4) and commands him to remove his sandals (v. 5, the second verse cited). Then he reveals himself to Moses as "the God of your father, the God of Abraham, the God of Isaac, and the God of Jacob," and Moses is afraid to look at God (*Elohim*) (v. 6). The confusion of the identities could hardly be more extreme: God first reveals himself as the angel of the Lord and then as God, and this God is alternately called *Elohim* and *YHWH*, whereas his angel carries the epithet *YHWH*.

Following mention of Metatron's other names, Rabbi Yehoshua cites additional relevant Bible verses. In the first verse quoted (Exod. 32:34), God clearly distinguishes between himself and his angel, but this is obviously the same angel as in the much-discussed verse Exodus 23:20, where the distinction was more ambiguous. A perfect example is then the next verse cited, Zechariah 3:2.[108] The impact only becomes obvious if we also consider the preceding verse, Zechariah 3:1: "Then he showed me the high priest Yehoshua[109] standing before the angel of the Lord (*mal'akh YHWH*), and Satan standing at his right hand to accuse him." Thus we again have the ambiguous situation that at first God's angel (Zech. 3:1) is mentioned and then God himself (Zech. 3:2: "And the Lord said to Satan"); hence the distinction is once again blurred. Making the confusion complete, this God (*YHWH*) again speaks of himself as God (*YHWH*). The critical apparatus of the *Biblia Hebraica* shows that the Peshitta, the Syriac translation of the Bible, renders the Hebrew *YHWH* in verse 2 as *mal'akh*

YHWH in order to avoid just this problem and harmonize the text.[110] There it is not God who is talking to Satan but rather the angel of the Lord (as in v. 1), who then announces God's rebuke of Satan.

The last verse cited, Genesis 19:24, is the well-known verse from the Babylonian Talmud, which also gives the impression that there are two Gods. This is followed by the appalled outcry, whether, God forbid, there might perhaps be two powers in heaven—similar to the perplexed outcry of Aher in the Bavli version of Elisha ben Avuyah's journey to heaven.[111] As in the Talmud, this suspicion is immediately rejected: in all the cited Bible verses, it turns out that we are not dealing with a second God but with an angel who carries God's name in his name, as we know from Exodus 23:21—that is, Metatron. Yet the verse is not explicitly cited here, which gives the author an opportunity to turn it around in a strange way: it is not the name of God that is contained in Metatron's name but vice versa, the name Metatron is in the name of God. I do not consider this a coincidence but instead—despite or even because of Metatron's degradation (Metatron is not a second divine power but merely an angel)—as an indirect, if not begrudging, valorization of Metatron.

All in all it is certainly correct, as Kister never tires of emphasizing, that this Geniza fragment as well as the other texts from the Hekhalot literature and the Bavli that we have discussed reject and oppose the idea of two Gods in heaven. But it is equally correct that this idea is part of Judaism and cannot simply be shunted off to Christianity. Kister's virtually desperate attempts to draw boundaries between a clearly defined rabbinic Judaism (which resisted binitarian temptations of any kind) and opponents outside this rabbinic Judaism, especially Christians,[112] ultimately paint a clear-cut, black-and-white picture that does justice neither to the relevant texts nor to the historical reality.[113]

CONCLUSION

Two Gods

OVER THE COURSE of its long history, Judaism has continuously wrestled with finding a way of expressing its notion of God with ever-greater precision. This applies to its founding document, the Hebrew Bible, as well as to all postbiblical literature. What we generally refer to today as monotheism is nothing more than an ideal that was pursued again and again, yet seldom achieved. Whereas YHWH, the tribal God of Israel, was never able to assert himself unchallenged even in the Hebrew Bible, the sources discussed here prove that also for postbiblical Judaism until far into late antiquity, the idea of one single God is an ideal—not only for authors of antiquity, but also for modern researchers—that does not stand up to an unbiased review. The Jewish heaven was by no means always content with one God, but, despite all trends to the contrary and manifold attempts to keep these trends at bay, was often populated with two Gods or a number of divine powers. The angels, originally demoted older divinities degraded to the status of servants, returned as divine figures next to the one and only God. Monotheism was to find its purest form in medieval Jewish philosophy, but there too had to confront the counter-movement of the Kabbalah, which became increasingly success-ful and popular. Not until the nineteenth century did monotheism become the generally valid norm, not least under the influence of Protestant Christianity. In a comparison of the three Abrahamic religions, it is Islam, however, that to this day represents the most uncompromising form of monotheism.

The two Gods of ancient Judaism are not antagonistic powers fighting against each other but instead rule peacefully with and next to one another. This is of course always on the assumption that one of the two is the ancestral "first" (as a rule, older) God of higher rank, who generously makes space in heaven next to and beneath him for the second (as a rule, younger) God. The "divinity" of this second God can be expressed in different degrees. A clear reference to a second "God" in the fullest sense of the word is avoided. Wherever the relationship to the "first" God is addressed directly, a "Son of God" or "Son of the Most High" is generally spoken of, and finally, as a culmination, a "Lesser" or "Younger God." For this reason I speak with caution of a "semidivine" figure beside God the creator. This reserve, however, must not belie the fact that our authors were always concerned with having this second godlike figure come as close as possible to the Most High God. The want for a second God is unmistakable.

The point of departure of almost all the traditions presented here is the Son of Man in the Book of Daniel. This Son of Man is an angel whose origin remains obscure or who was always in heaven with God, prior to Creation. As such, he is raised to a godlike or semidivine figure, who as a savior/redeemer/Messiah is closely tied to the fate of the people of Israel. Yet the Son of Man can also be a human being who ascends from earth to heaven, is transformed there into an angel, takes his place next to God, and will return to earth as Israel's redeemer. These two lines of the divinized angel and divinized human overlap, and cannot always be clearly distinguished from one another. In both cases, the divinization of the angel or human is not an end in itself but always serves a redeemer function.

The proximity of binitarian ideas of pre-Christian ancient Judaism to thoughts and images as encountered in the New Testament is obvious. This is not merely a matter of parallels, much less equations, but rather of the fundamental insight that Second Temple Judaism prepared the stock on which the New Testament could draw. The fact that this, apart from many other themes, also applies to the notion of a "second" God next to the "first" God is an insight that is only slowly beginning to gain acceptance.

The New Testament's recourse to Second Temple Judaism, however, represents neither a simple transfer nor a completely new creation. In the process of adopting early Jewish traditions, bounds are overstepped and shifted, and new boundaries are drawn; extreme care is necessary in dealing with the sources in order to avoid rash conclusions and new clichés.

The most striking difference between the binitarian ideas of postexilic Judaism and the Christology of the New Testament is that in Second Temple Judaism, the godlike or semidivine figure next to God never becomes a human being. He can be a human, but is never a second "God" who must become "human" in order to complete his mission of redemption on earth. This is reserved for Christianity. The humanness of the "human" who becomes "God" in Judaism is extinguished and no longer has any meaning for his mission on earth. In Christianity, on the other hand, the incarnation of God is a basic component in the process of redemption. Any attempt to blur this distinction overshoots by far the mark of a proper analysis of the sources.

The divinization of a human being is taken the furthest in the Similitudes of the Ethiopic Book of Enoch and the Third Book of Enoch. The climax of this development is the designation of the human Enoch, who is transformed into the angel Metatron and divine vice-regent, as a "Lesser/Younger God" (*YHWH ha-qatan*). This epithet was regarded as so bold, even in 3 Enoch itself, that the redactor felt compelled to immediately counter the elevation of Enoch-Metatron to *YHWH ha-qatan* by citing a source in which Metatron is degraded to an ordinary angel. The inclusion and harsh rejection of such ideas in the Babylonian Talmud serve to show how widespread as well as feared they were in the rabbinic

Judaism of Babylonia. Other texts in the Hekhalot literature prove to be less sensitive here.

It is conspicuous that binitarian ideas are concentrated in Babylonian Judaism. Here the Babylonian Talmud and the Hekhalot literature of early Jewish mysticism—regardless of the degree of acceptance and/or rejection—obviously derive from the same sources. I assume, therefore, that the idea of two Gods experienced a new heyday not in Palestinian but in Babylonian Judaism, and that this is related to the role that Christianity played in these two Jewish centers. Whereas Christianity in Palestine distinguished itself more and more at the expense of Judaism, and ultimately became the state religion in the Roman Empire, Christians in the Persian Sasanian Empire remained more peripheral, and in stark contrast to the Jews, were even persecuted as supporters of the Byzantine Empire. Consequently, Babylonian Jews could, more easily than their coreligionists in Palestine, hark back to their own, genuinely Jewish traditions that had meanwhile become the trademark of Christianity.

In the development of binitarian ideas from Daniel to early Jewish mysticism, to the extent that their historical verification is reasonably reliable, I have drafted a trajectory that does not proceed linearly but rather indicates distortions and breaches. All attempts to span the vast time frame from the second century BCE to the seventh/ninth century CE through the construction of an "Enochic Judaism" anchored in Jewish mysticism are misguided. Neither can the figure of Enoch be used as a bracket encompassing such different and chronologically distant books as the Similitudes of the First Book of Enoch (which were composed around the turn of the eras) and the Third Book of Enoch (whose final editing took place between 600 and 900 CE), nor can these books be summarized under the common denominator of a "Jewish mysticism" that traces itself back to pre-Christian Judaism. Furthermore, taking up Enoch as the protagonist of an ostensibly mystical and thus by definition less "law"-oriented Judaism is theologically and methodologically extremely problematic. It is just as unsatisfactory to revive the chimera of an apocalyptic trend that extends from the early Jewish apocrypha and pseudepigrapha to far into rabbinic Judaism, in order to create a bridge between the binitarian ideas of pre-Christian and rabbinic Judaism. Whether we like it or not, the Jews of Palestine reject the beautiful picture of an unbroken line of binitarian tradition through all ancient and late antique Judaism.

It is precisely on this point that I distinguish myself from research up to now and in particular from the picture drafted by Daniel Boyarin, who apart from me has dealt with these traditions in greater detail. We agree that binitarian ideas are firmly anchored in Second Temple Judaism. But we do not concur in our assessment of the further development in the first centuries CE. Nothing lies further from my intentions than to postulate a fundamental difference between "Judaism" and "Christianity" in late antiquity. Quite the contrary, early Christianity and rabbinic Judaism are not two "religions" that were firmly established from the outset; rather, they only gradually crystallized in an extended process and in discourse with and against each other, with considerable differences between this new rabbinic Judaism and the Judaism of the Second Temple period. If I characterize the binitarian ideas of 3 Enoch and the Bavli that took shape at the end of this process also as a response to the New Testament message of Jesus Christ, then by no means am I questioning the fact that this answer has its Jewish roots in pre-Christian times. Again, on the contrary, the response is an original Jewish one, but I doubt that the authors of 3 Enoch and the Bavli consciously placed themselves within this pre-Christian Jewish tradition (that is, that they knew it literarily); and I assume that they reacted primarily to the adaptation of this tradition through Christianity, which had meanwhile become firmly established. The Jewish answer to Christianity is a *Jewish* answer insofar as it refers back to the eminently Jewish traditions as they are preserved in the rich literature of the Second Temple period. And it is also a response to *Christianity* insofar as it directly confronts the shape that these traditions assumed in the New Testament and early Christian literature.

ABBREVIATIONS

b	Babylonian Talmud (Bavli)
b.	ben (son of)
Cant.	Canticles (also Song of Songs, or Song of Solomon)
col.	column
Col.	Epistle to the Colossians
Dan.	Daniel
Deut.	Deuteronomy
DJD	*Discoveries in the Judaean Desert*
DSD	*Dead Sea Discoveries*
Eccles.	Ecclesiastes (Kohelet)
1 Enoch	1st (Ethiopic) Book of Enoch
2 Enoch	2nd (Slavonic) Book of Enoch
3 Enoch	3rd (Hebrew) Book of Enoch
Exod.	Exodus
Ezek.	Ezekiel
FJB	*Frankfurter Judaistische Beiträge*
fol.	folio
Gen.	Genesis
Heb.	Epistle to the Hebrews
Hos.	Hosea
HTR	*Harvard Theological Review*
Isa.	Isaiah
Jer.	Jeremiah
JJS	*Journal of Jewish Studies*
John	Gospel of John
JPS	*Jewish Publication Society*
JSJ	*Journal for the Study of Judaism*
JSQ	*Jewish Studies Quarterly*
JTS	*Journal of Theological Studies*
Jude	Epistle of Jude
1 Kings	1st Book of Kings

2 Kings	2nd Book of Kings
Luke	Gospel of Luke
Mark	Gospel of Mark
Matt.	Gospel of Matthew
MS	Manuscript
MSS	Manuscripts
PG	*Patrologia Graeca*
Prov.	Proverbs
Ps.	Psalms
Ps. Sol.	Psalms of Solomon
RdQ	*Revue de Qumran*
Rev. (or Apoc.)	Revelation of John or Apocalypse of John
RGG	*Religion in Geschichte und Gegenwart*
2 Sam.	2nd Book of Samuel
TRE	*Theologische Realenzyklopädie*
TUAT	*Texte aus der Umwelt des Alten Testaments*
v.	verse
Wisd. of Sol.	Wisdom of Solomon (*Sapientia Salomonis*)
y	Jerusalem Talmud (*Yerushalmi*)
Zech.	Zechariah

NOTES

Introduction: One God?

1. The first radical yet only temporarily successful attempt at a "monotheistic counterrevolution" has been attributed to the ill-fated pharaoh Amenhotep IV (Akhenaten). For a detailed exploration, which triggered a broad and controversial discussion, see Jan Assmann, *Moses the Egyptian: The Memory of Egypt in Western Monotheism* (Cambridge, MA: Harvard University Press, 1997).

2. An early, lone critic of the cliché of Jewish monotheism was Peter Hayman. For his now-classic article, see Peter Hayman, "Monotheism—A Misused Word in Jewish Studies?" *JJS* 42 (1991): 1–15.

3. For just a selection of the many relevant articles, see Gregor Ahn, "Monotheismus und Polytheismus I: Religionswissenschaftlich," in *RGG*, ed. Hans Dieter Betz, Don S. Browning, Bernd Janowski, and Eberhard Jüngel (Tübingen: Mohr Siebeck, ⁴2002), vol. 5, cols. 1457–59; Hans-Peter Müller, "Monotheismus und Polytheismus II: Altes Testament," in *RGG*, ed. Hans Dieter Betz, Don S. Browning, Bernd Janowski, and Eberhard Jüngel (Tübingen: Mohr Siebeck, ⁴2002), vol. 5, cols. 1459–62. For one of the most important recent books on biblical monotheism, see Mark S. Smith, *The Origins of Biblical Monotheism: Israel's Polytheistic Background and the Ugaritic Texts* (Oxford: Oxford University Press, 2001). I myself also dealt with this topic in the introduction to my book *Mirror of His Beauty: Feminine Images of God from the Bible to the Early Kabbalah* (Princeton, NJ: Princeton University Press, 2002), 1ff.

4. In Deut. 32:8–10, YHWH is still subordinate to the "Most High" god (El), whereas in Ps. 89:6–8, he appears as head of the divine council.

5. Otto Kaiser, ed., *TUAT*, vol. 2, *Religiöse Texte: Grab-, Sarg-, Votiv- und Bauinschriften*, ed. Christel Butterweck et al. (Gütersloh: Mohn, 1988), 563–64.

6. On Judah, see 1 Kings 15:13. On Israel, see 1 Kings 16:32–33; 2 Kings 10:18ff. On Jerusalem, see 2 Kings 21:3–7.

7. Müller, "Monotheismus und Polytheismus II," *RGG*, vol. 5, col. 1461.

8. Müller, ibid.

9. Less common terms are "ditheistic" and "ditheism."

10. R. Travers Hereford, *Christianity in Talmud and Midrash*, (1903; exp. ed., Jersey City, NJ: Ktav, 2006); Alan F. Segal, *Two Powers in Heaven: Early Rabbinic Reports about Christianity and Gnosticism* (Leiden: Brill, 1977).

11. Daniel Boyarin, *Border Lines: The Partition of Judaeo-Christianity* (Philadelphia: University of Pennsylvania Press, 2004).

12. Daniel Boyarin, "The Gospel of the Memra: Jewish Binitarianism and the Prologue to John," *HTR* 94 (2001): 243–84; idem, "Two Powers in Heaven; or, The Making of a Heresy," in *The Idea of Biblical Interpretation: Essays in Honor of James L. Kugel*, ed. Hindy Najman and Judith H. Newman (Leiden: Brill, 2004), 331–70; idem, "The Parables of Enoch and the Foundation of the Rabbinic Sect: A Hypothesis," in *"The Words of a Wise Man's Mouth Are Gracious" (Qoh 10,12): Festschrift for Günter Stemberger on the Occasion of His 65th Birthday*, ed. Mauro Perani (Berlin: Walter de Gruyter, 2005), 53–72; idem, "Beyond Judaisms: Meṭaṭron and the Divine Polymorphy of Ancient Judaism," *JSJ* 41 (2010): 323–65; idem, "Once Again: 'Two Dominions in Heaven' in the Mekhilta," *Tarbiz* 81 (2012–13): 87–101 (Hebr.); idem, "Is Metatron a Converted Christian?" *Judaïsme Ancien / Ancient Judaism* 1 (2013): 13–62.

13. Peter Schäfer, *Die Geburt des Judentums aus dem Geist des Christentums. Fünf Vorlesungen zur Entstehung des rabbinischen Judentums* (Tübingen: Mohr Siebeck, 2010); idem, *The Jewish Jesus: How Judaism and Christianity Shaped Each Other* (Princeton, NJ: Princeton University Press, 2012). Although it appeared later than *Die Geburt des Judentums*, *The Jewish Jesus* is the (more comprehensive) original version, which was abridged for the Jena lectures and which I translated into German. My methodological premises in *The Jewish Jesus* are developed more programmatically and in much greater detail (see especially the introduction) than in *Die Geburt des Judentums*. Boyarin's article "Is Metatron a Converted Christian?" is to a large degree a discussion of my book *The Jewish Jesus*.

14. Menahem Kister, "The Manifestations of God in the Midrashic Literature in Light of Christian Texts," *Tarbiz* 81 (2012–13): 103–42 (Hebr.); idem, "Metatron, God, and the 'Two Powers': The Dynamics of Tradition, Exegesis, and Polemic," *Tarbiz* 82 (2013–14): 43–88 (Hebr.).

15. Originally his 1973 inaugural lecture at the University of Tübingen, this has been published in numerous versions in German and English, most recently as "Der Sohn Gottes," in Martin Hengel, *Studien zur Christologie. Kleine Schriften IV* (Tübingen: Mohr Siebeck, 2006), 74–145. See also Martin Hengel, *The Son of God: The Origin of Christology and the History of Jewish Hellenistic Religion*, trans. John Bowden (1976; repr., Eugene, OR: Wipf and Stock, 2007). Although closely focused on the Messiah, nevertheless helpful for our topic is John J. Collins, *The Scepter and the Star: The Messiahs of the Dead Sea Scrolls and Other Ancient Literature* (New York: Doubleday, 1995). The second edition appeared with a new subtitle and a completely new

chapter 6 on the heavenly throne; see John J. Collins, *The Scepter and the Star: Messianism in Light of the Dead Sea Scrolls*, 2nd ed. (Grand Rapids, MI: Eerdmans, 2010).

16. The literature in this area has become virtually boundless. Here I will limit myself largely to Larry W. Hurtado and Richard Bauckham, the two main actors dominating this field. Larry W. Hurtado opened the discussion with *One God, One Lord: Early Christian Devotion and Ancient Jewish Monotheism* (London: SCM Press, 1988), followed by idem, *How on Earth Did Jesus Become a God?: Historical Questions about Earliest Devotion to Jesus* (Grand Rapids, MI: Eerdmans, 2005) and idem, *God in New Testament Theology* (Nashville, TN: Abingdon, 2010). Richard Bauckham developed his theories for the first time in the much-acclaimed essay *God Crucified: Monotheism and Christology in the New Testament* (Grand Rapids, MI: Eerdmans, 1998), which he expanded a decade later with additional explorations into what he considers a prolegomenon of a "Christology of divine identity." See idem, *Jesus and the God of Israel: God Crucified and Other Studies on the New Testament's Christology of Divine Identity* (Grand Rapids, MI: Eerdmans, 2008).

17. The latter is represented with particular vigor by Margaret Barker. See especially Margaret Barker, *The Great Angel: A Study of Israel's Second God* (London: SPCK, 1992); eadem, *The Great High Priest: The Temple Roots of Christian Liturgy* (London: T & T Clark, 2003). For a Judaism scholar focused on religious history, these books are particularly hard to digest. They contain numerous surprising as well as brilliant insights, but all in all create a new syncretistic religion that avoids any and all chronological, geographic, and literary differentiations.

18. That is, for both (as well as for most Christian theological authors), the actual binitarian revolution is reserved for Christianity.

19. The similarities and differences between Hurtado and Bauckham, in their dialogue with other researchers, become especially clear in two major essays that were contributions in Festschriften. See Richard Bauckham, "Devotion to Jesus Christ in Earliest Christianity: An Appraisal and Discussion of the Work of Larry Hurtado," in *Mark, Manuscripts, and Monotheism: Essays in Honor of Larry W. Hurtado*, ed. Chris Keith and Dieter T. Roth (London: Bloomsbury, 2015), 176–200; Larry W. Hurtado, "Richard Bauckham's Christological Pilgrimage," in *In the Fullness of Time: Essays on Christology, Creation, and Eschatology in Honor of Richard Bauckham*, ed. Daniel M. Gurtner, Grant Macaskill, and Jonathan T. Pennington (Grand Rapids, MI: Eerdmans, 2016), 82–96.

20. Daniel Boyarin, *The Jewish Gospels: The Story of the Jewish Christ* (New York: New Press, 2012).

21. Peter Schäfer, "The Jew Who Would Be God," *New Republic*, June 7, 2012, 36–39. After that, I examined and further developed this part of the subject in several lectures (at Yale University, as the Wellhausen lecture at the University of Göttingen, at the Israel Institute for Advanced Studies at the Hebrew University

of Jerusalem, as the Dalman lecture in Greifswald, in the Berlin Antike-Kolleg, and at the University of Vienna). The diverse audiences helped me refine my thoughts and sharpen my theses—and sometimes retract them, if I had ventured too far.

22. For a critical appraisal of "Early High Christology," which is closely related to my considerations, see Philip S. Alexander, " 'The Agent of the King Is Treated as the King Himself': Does the Worship of Jesus Imply His Divinity?" in *In the Fullness of Time: Essays on Christology, Creation, and Eschatology in Honor of Richard Bauckham*, ed. Daniel M. Gurtner, Grant Macaskill, and Jonathan T. Pennington (Grand Rapids, MI: Eerdmanns, 2016), 97–114.

23. Matt. 26:63–64; Luke 22:67; Mark 14:62.

24. The editors of the Babylonian Talmud were not bothered by the fact that the historical Aqiva was a representative of *Palestinian* Judaism.

Chapter 1: The Son of Man in the Vision of Daniel

1. For the sake of simplicity, in the following I also use the commonly used phrase "Son of Man."

2. Frank Moore Cross, *Canaanite Myth and Hebrew Epic* (Cambridge, MA: Harvard University Press, 1973), 43.

3. Daniel Boyarin, "Daniel 7, Intertextuality, and the History of Israel's Cult," *HTR* 105, no. 2 (2012): 139–62.

4. Michael Segal, *Dreams, Riddles, and Visions: Textual, Contextual, and Intertextual Approaches to the Book of Daniel* (Berlin: de Gruyter, 2016). Through the good offices of Professor Reinhard Kratz, Segal was kind enough to grant me access to the fourth chapter of his book manuscript ("Reconsidering the Theological Background of Daniel 7 and 4Q246 in Light of Innerbiblical Interpretation"), and I had the opportunity to discuss this chapter with him in detail in Jerusalem. He has meanwhile published the part on the Daniel Apocryphon separately (see below).

5. The same conclusion was already drawn by John Emerton: "There are good grounds for believing that the enthronement of the Son of man by an aged deity goes back to Canaanite myth and ritual, and that behind the figure of the Son of man lies Yahwe, and ultimately Baal." John A. Emerton, "The Origin of the Son of Man Imagery," *JTS* 9 (1958): 242. I would like to thank my colleague Martha Himmelfarb for drawing my attention to this important contribution.

6. In my opinion, John Collins overemphasizes the angels as a collective distinct from Israel. This is not a matter of either-or (either the angels or Israel) but instead a combination of the two: the dominion is given not to the angels but to Israel as an angel-like community, similar to the meaning of Israel in Qumran. See John J. Collins, *Daniel: A Commentary on the Book of Daniel* (Minneapolis: Fortress Press, 1993), 313–19.

7. Boyarin, "Daniel 7," 154ff.

8. Supposedly the *peshar*, followed by most exegetes, already interprets the "one like a human being" as a symbol of the people of Israel (Boyarin, "Daniel 7," 140–41) and transfers this symbolic reading to the vision, with the goal of demythologizing and tempering the original Daniel text. What Boyarin presents here is a classical two-sources theory, inspired by the outmoded and, in this form, problematic theory of multiple sources of German Old Testament scholarship. Collins (*Daniel*, 305) speaks of a "mythic-realistic symbol for God, the Ancient One, [who] is assumed to exist outside the dream."

9. Boyarin is not the first to claim this. See John J. Collins, *The Scepter and the Star: The Messiahs of the Dead Sea Scrolls and Other Ancient Literature* (New York: Doubleday, 1995), 142 (only in the 1st ed., deleted in the 2nd ed.). Collins also refers to the Babylonian Talmud.

10. See pp. 81ff. below.

11. Boyarin has meanwhile acknowledged this ("Is Metatron a Converted Christian?" *Judaïsme Ancien / Ancient Judaism* 1 [2013]: 33n39), but he does wish to localize the two thrones in the parallel account, *Mekhilta de-Rabbi Shimon ben Yochai* (Jacob Nahum Epstein and Ezra Zion Melamed, eds., *Mekhilta de-Rabbi Shimon ben Yochai* [Jerusalem: Mekize Nirdamim, 1955], 233). Again, I cannot follow this, as this parallel also does nothing but introduce Exodus 15:3 as proof text for the young war god and Daniel 7:9 as proof text for the Ancient One, as does the Mekhilta de-Rabbi Ishmael. I find it puzzling how Boyarin ("Metatron," 33n39) comes to the conclusion, "Although it is not absolutely proven that the problem of the two thrones is what lies at the heart of this passage, so close to our Mekhilta, I find such a reading extremely attractive indeed, nearly inescapable, if not entirely so" (ibid.). The rhetoric here is all too obvious.

12. With this I am attempting to take up the approaches of *both* Segal *and* Boyarin, and place them in a historically reliable perspective.

13. Collins, *Daniel*, 304–411. See also idem, *The Scepter and the Star: Messianism in Light of the Dead Sea Scrolls*, 2nd ed. (Grand Rapids, MI: Eerdmans, 2010), 195.

14. Daniel 8:15 (*gaver*); 8:16, 10:18 (*adam*); 10:16 (*bene adam*); 9:21, 10:5 (*ish*).

15. The same wording as in Dan. 10:18, which clearly refers to an angel.

16. Boyarin, "Daniel 7," 149.

17. Read *ish* instead of *esh*.

Chapter 2: The Personified Wisdom in the Wisdom Literature

1. Here I am summarizing and modifying what I wrote in my book *Mirror of His Beauty: Feminine Images of God from the Bible to the Early Kabbalah* (Princeton, NJ: Princeton University Press, 2002), 19–38.

2. David Andrew Teeter and Bernd U. Schipper, eds., *Wisdom and Torah: The Reception of "Torah" in the Wisdom Literature of the Second Temple Period* (Leiden: Brill, 2013).

3. Literally: "poured out."

4. For an overview, see Bernhard Lang, *Frau Weisheit. Deutung einer biblischen Gestalt* (Düsseldorf: Patmos, 1975), 93ff.; Otto Plöger, *Sprüche Salomos (Proverbia)* (Neukirchen-Vluyn: Neukirchener Verlag, 1984), 86–87, 94ff.

5. See also Wisd. of Sol. 7:21–22, 8:6: *technitis* (fashioner or craftswoman).

6. See Christa Kayatz, *Studien zu Proverbien 1–9. Eine form- und motivgeschicht-liche Untersuchung unter Einbeziehung ägyptischen Vergleichsmaterials* (Neukirchen-Vluyn: Neukirchener Verlag, 1966), 93ff.; Burton L. Mack, *Logos und Sophia. Untersu-chungen zur Weisheitstheologie im hellenistischen Judentum* (Göttingen: Vandenhoeck and Ruprecht, 1973), 34ff.; Jan Assmann, *Ma'at. Gerechtigkeit und Unsterblichkeit im Alten Ägypten* (Munich: Beck, 1990).

7. Literally "vapor, mist" (*atmis*).

8. And not, as it is often translated, "in/with wisdom."

9. FragmT Gen. 1:1 (MS Paris). See Michael L. Klein, ed., *The Fragment-Targums of the Pentateuch according to Their Extant Sources*, vol. 1, *Text, Indices, and Introductory Essays* (Rome: Biblical Institute Press, 1980), 43; idem, ed., *The Fragment-Targums of the Pentateuch according to Their Extant Sources*, vol. 2, *Translations* (Rome: Biblical Institute Press, 1980), 3. A marginal gloss corrects *be-hokhmah* to the more common *min leqadmin*—"in the beginning." MS Vatican also has *be-hokhmah*, but leaves out "and perfected" (Klein, *Fragment-Targums*, 1:126, 2:90).

10. Genesis Rabbah 1:1.

11. Alejandro Díez Macho, *Neophyti 1: Targum Palestinense MS de la Biblioteca Vaticana*, vol. 1: *Génesis: Edición Príncipe, Introducción General y Versión Castellana* (Madrid: Consejo Superior de Investigaciones Científicas, 1968), 3.

12. Anonymous, *The Palestinian Targum to the Pentateuch: Codex Vatican (Neo-fiti 1)* (Jerusalem: Makor, 1970), 2. Hence the verse Genesis 1:1 originally read as follows: *Mileqadmin be-hokhmah bera de-YYY' we-shakhlel yat shemayya ve-yat ar'a.*

13. Díez Macho, *Neophyti 1*, 57ff.; Peter Schäfer, "Bibelübersetzungen II: Targu-min," in *TRE*, ed. Gerhard Krause and Gerhard Müller (Tübingen: Mohr Siebeck, 1980), 6:217.

14. Martin McNamara, *Targum Neofiti 1: Genesis*, The Aramaic Bible, Volume 1A (Collegeville, MN: Michael Glazier, 1992), 45.

15. This explanation was already suggested by Díez Macho, *Neophyti 1*, 3, critical apparatus to Gen. 1:1. See also McNamara, *Targum Neofiti 1*, 52n2.

16. A glance into the related weblogs makes it easy to see how dangerous such an option was and is viewed to be.

Chapter 3: The Divinized Human in the Self-Glorification Hymn from Qumran

1. Quoted with minor editing, from Esther Eshel, "4Q471B: A Self-Glorification Hymn," *RdQ* 17/65–68 (1996): 184–85. See also the German translation by Johann Maier, *Die Qumran-Essener. Die Texte vom Toten Meer* (Munich: Ernst Reinhardt Verlag, 1995), 2:559–60.

2. Or, "of the East" (as in Maier, ibid.).

3. For a more comprehensive analysis, see Peter Schäfer, *The Origins of Jewish Mysticism* (Princeton, NJ: Princeton University Press, 2011), 146ff.

4. 4Q471^b, fragments 1–2, line 5; 4Q427 (4QH^a), fragment 7, col. 1, line 8.

5. As has been correctly observed by Eshel, "4Q471B," 180.

6. There are close parallels in the hymns of praise, the Hodayot. On this, see John J. Collins, *The Scepter and the Star: Messianism in Light of the Dead Sea Scrolls*, 2nd ed. (Grand Rapids, MI: Eerdmans, 2010), 150–51.

7. I am herewith correcting my statement in *The Origins of Jewish Mysticism*, 147–48.

8. 1QM, xvii, 7.

9. Maurice Baillet, *Qumrân Grotte 4.3 (4Q482–4Q520). DJD-7* (Oxford: Clarendon Press, 1982), 7:26–30.

10. Morton Smith, "Two Ascended to Heaven: Jesus and the Author of 4Q491," in *Jesus and the Dead Sea Scrolls*, ed. James H. Charlesworth, 290–301 (New York: Doubleday, 1992), 298.

11. Collins, *The Scepter and the Star*, 2nd ed., 159. See also, similarly, Eshel, "4Q471B," 202.

12. Schäfer, *The Origins of Jewish Mysticism*, 150.

13. Schäfer, ibid., 150–51.

14. Collins, *The Scepter and the Star*, 2nd ed., 164.

15. Israel Knohl, *The Messiah before Jesus: The Suffering Servant of the Dead Sea Scrolls* (Berkeley: University of California Press, 2000), 42ff.

Chapter 4: The Son of God and Son of the Most High in the Daniel Apocryphon from Qumran

1. For a good summary, see John J. Collins, *The Scepter and the Star: Messianism in Light of the Dead Sea Scrolls*, 2nd ed. (Grand Rapids, MI: Eerdmans, 2010), 171ff.

2. Florentino García Martínez and Eibert J. C. Tigchelaar, eds., *The Dead Sea Scrolls Study Edition* (Leiden: Brill, 1997), 492–95.

3. Here and in the following, the antecedent is either the Son of God / Son of the Most High (here, *he/him/his*) or the people (here, *it/its*) of God.

4. Michael Segal, "Who Is the 'Son of God' in 4Q246? An Overlooked Example of Early Biblical Interpretation," *DSD* 21 (2014): 301.

5. Frank Moore Cross, *The Ancient Library at Qumran* (Sheffield, UK: Sheffield Academic Press; Minneapolis, MN: Fortress Press, 1995), 190–91; idem, "The Structure of the Apocalypse of 'Son of God' (4Q246)," in *Emanuel: Studies in Hebrew Bible, Septuagint, and Dead Sea Scrolls in Honor of Emanuel Tov*, ed. Shalom M. Paul, Robert A. Kraft, Lawrence H. Schiffman, and Weston W. Fields (Leiden: Brill, 2003), 151–58; Collins, *The Scepter and the Star*, 2nd ed., 173ff.

6. For emphasis on an eschatological savior figure, see Florentino García Martínez, "The Eschatological Figure of 4Q246," in *Qumran and Apocalyptic: Studies on the Aramaic Texts from Qumran* (Leiden: Brill, 1992), 173; idem, "Two Messianic Figures in the Qumran Texts," in *Current Research and Technological Developments on the Dead Sea Scrolls: Conference on the Texts from the Judean Desert, Jerusalem, 30 April 1995*, ed. Donald W. Parry and Stephen D. Ricks (Leiden: Brill, 1996), 25ff.

7. 11Q13, ii, 9–10.

8. Common translations level this out even more by eliminating the difference between *Elohim* and *El*: "God stands in the divine assembly; among the divine beings He pronounces judgment" (JPS).

9. 11Q13, ii, 24–25. Although "Melchizedek" has been added, it is clear from the context that he is meant, as he will liberate Zion from the hand of Belial.

10. 11Q13, ii, 11; remarkably, what is rendered here as "El" is actually "YHWH" in the Masoretic Text of the Hebrew Bible.

11. 11Q13, ii, 13.

12. Józef Milik interprets this as divine hypostasis. See Józef T. Milik, "'Milkî-ṣedek et Milkî-reša' dans les anciens écrits juifs et chrétiens," *JJS* 23 (1972): 95–144.

13. 1QM, xi, 17.

14. 1QM, xiii, 10.

15. 1QM, xvii, 6–7.

16. García Martínez ("Two Messianic Figures in the Qumran Texts," 30) speaks of "a messiah, an almost divinized messiah, similar to Melchizedek and the heavenly Son of Man." Collins (*The Scepter and the Star*, 2nd ed., 181ff.) distinguishes too schematically between the collective, the angelic, and the messianic interpretations. The individual lines of interpretation cannot always be clearly separated but often overlap.

17. Luke 1:31.

18. Cross, *The Ancient Library*, 190; idem, "The Structure of the Apocalypse," 157n20. For a summary, see Segal, "Who Is the 'Son of God' in 4Q246?" 302–3.

19. On this, see Collins, *The Scepter and the Star*, 2nd ed., 171ff. David Flusser goes yet a step further and votes for the Antichrist. See David Flusser, "The Hubris of the Antichrist in a Fragment from Qumran," *Immanuel* 10 (1980): 31–37; idem, *Judaism and the Origins of Christianity* (Jerusalem: Magnes Press, 1998), 207–13.

20. Segal, "Who Is the 'Son of God' in 4Q246?," 311.

21. Segal, ibidem, 301.

22. Better: II, 1, the passage in question.

23. Segal overlooks the fact that the *vacat* is not only at the beginning but also at the end of line II, 4. Thus I think it serves not so much to mark the transition from the negative to the positive narrative thread (Segal, "Who is the 'Son of God,' " 300), but instead emphasizes the salvation-historical importance of the people of God.

24. Adela Yarbro Collins and John J. Collins, *King and Messiah as Son of God: Divine, Human, and Angelic Messianic Figures in Biblical and Related Literature* (Grand Rapids, MI: Eerdmans, 2008), 70–71.

25. See also Collins, *The Scepter and the Star*, 2nd ed., 177: "The description of the conflict between the peoples in column 2 is redundant, but such redundancy is a feature of apocalyptic style."

26. Segal, "Who Is the 'Son of God' in 4Q246?" 298, 301.

27. See also Collins, *The Scepter and the Star*, 2nd ed., 172.

28. See also Collins, ibidem, 178: "The ambiguity of the third person suffixes in column 2 of our Qumran fragment can be explained most satisfactorily if the one who is called 'Son of God' is understood as the ruler or representative of the people of God. The everlasting kingdom, then, belongs to both, and the 'Son of God' exercises universal judgment on behalf of his people." Collins, however, then takes a step back and warns against emphasizing the parallel with Daniel too strongly. Similarly ambivalent is the appraisal when he resumes the subject in Collins and Collins, *King and Messiah as Son of God*, 72–73. On the one hand, he stresses the link in the tradition history to the Son of Man in Daniel 7, but on the other hand, he downplays this by arguing that the Daniel Apocryphon is certainly not an interpretation of Daniel 7. Yet both might in fact be closely connected with regard to tradition history, without the entire text having to be viewed as an interpretation of Daniel 7. Here as well, Collins is thinking too schematically in predefined categories.

Chapter 5: The Son of Man–Enoch in the Similitudes of the Ethiopic Book of Enoch

1. The translation follows George W. E. Nickelsburg and James C. VanderKam, eds., *1 Enoch: The Hermeneia Translation* (Minneapolis: Fortress Press, 2012), 59–60, 62.

2. John J. Collins, *The Scepter and the Star: Messianism in Light of the Dead Sea Scrolls*, 2nd ed. (Grand Rapids, MI: Eerdmans, 2010), 200. Collins here refers to Psalm 147:4, where God gives the stars their names—that is, he creates them. In the following, I will avoid the word "preexisting" because it suggests uncreated, eternal existence. The son of man, although he exists prior to the creation of the world, is created and consequently not eternal.

3. Nickelsburg and VanderKam, *1 Enoch*, 62.

4. Also for Collins (*The Scepter and the Star*, 2nd ed., 204n61), the veneration and worship of the Son of Man is the most natural reading.

5. 1 Enoch 58–69.

6. 1 Enoch 69:26–29. This portion probably belongs with Enoch 63–64.

7. Thus it is written in the third person in the text. In the following, the narrative switches to the first person: Enoch now tells about himself. This too could be an indication of a literary seam.

8. 1 Enoch 71:5ff.

9. Daniel Boyarin, *The Jewish Gospels: The Story of the Jewish Christ* (New York: New Press, 2012), 88.

10. Moshe Idel, *Ben: Sonship and Jewish Mysticism* (London: Continuum, 2007), 4.

11. Boyarin, *The Jewish Gospels*, 85.

12. Boyarin, ibidem, 94.

Chapter 6: The Son of Man–Messiah in the Fourth Book of Ezra

1. Here I continue the discussion that I started in Peter Schäfer, *Die Geburt des Judentums aus dem Geist des Christentums. Fünf Vorlesungen zur Entstehung des rabbinischen Judentums* (Tübingen: Mohr Siebeck, 2010), 89ff.; and in idem, *The Jewish Jesus: How Judaism and Christianity Shaped Each Other* (Princeton, NJ: Princeton University Press, 2012), 78–79.

2. 4 Ezra 13:2ff. The translation follows B. M. Metzger, "The Fourth Book of Ezra," in *The Old Testament Pseudepigrapha*, ed. James H. Charlesworth (New York: Doubleday, 1983), 1:517–59. It is irrelevant for our context whether or not the vision in 4 Ezra 13 was originally an independent tradition, to which the author of 4 Ezra added his own interpretation, as suggested by Michael E. Stone, *Features of the Eschatology of IV Ezra* (Atlanta, GA: Scholars Press, 1989), 123ff.; idem, *Fourth Ezra: A Commentary on the Book of Fourth Ezra* (Minneapolis: Fortress Press, 1990), 211ff.

3. As the rabbis understood Deuteronomy 33:2 (*esh dat, a fire of law*).

4. Odil H. Steck, *Israel und das gewaltsame Geschick der Propheten. Untersuchungen zur Überlieferung des deuteronomistischen Geschichtsbildes im Alten Testament, Spätjudentum und Urchristentum* (Neukirchen-Vluyn: Neukirchener Verlag, 1967), 177ff.

5. The ten tribes might also be a rabbinic reminiscence.

6. In 13:37, both Arabic translations have "my youth."

7. Josef Schreiner, *Das 4. Buch Esra*. Jüdische Schriften aus hellenistisch-römischer Zeit, vol. 5, *Apokalypsen* (Gütersloh: Gütersloher Verlagshaus Gerd Mohn, 1981), 397n32a.

8. Septuagint: *hyios*; Vulgate: *filius*.

9. Collins refers to him as a "preexistent … transcendent figure of heavenly origin." John J. Collins, *The Scepter and the Star: Messianism in Light of the Dead Sea Scrolls*, 2nd ed. (Grand Rapids, MI: Eerdmans, 2010), 210.

10. Michael Stone (*Fourth Ezra*, 383) points out that fire is mentioned in 4 Ezra only in connection with God. The sole exception is 4 Ezra 13:10. As mentioned above, fire comes out of the mouth of the Messiah—a further indication of the special status of the godlike Messiah in 4 Ezra 13.

Chapter 7: The Firstborn in the Prayer of Joseph

1. For an English translation with a comprehensive introduction, see Jonathan Z. Smith, "Prayer of Joseph," in *The Old Testament Pseudepigrapha*, ed. James H. Charlesworth (New York: Doubleday, 1985), 2:699–714.

2. Smith, ibidem, 713.

3. The Greek word *archikos* can mean both "ruling" and "original, primordially eternal."

4. Smith, "Prayer of Joseph," 713.

5. Martin Hengel, *The Son of God: The Origin of Christology and the History of Jewish Hellenistic Religion*, trans. John Bowden (1976; repr., Eugene, OR: Wipf and Stock, 2007), 48.

6. Jonathan Z. Smith, "The Prayer of Joseph," in *Religions in Antiquity: Essays in Memory of Erwin Ramsdell Goodenough*, ed. Jacob Neusner (Leiden: Brill, 1968), 272.

Chapter 8: The Logos according to Philo of Alexandria

1. On this in greater detail, see Peter Schäfer, *Mirror of His Beauty: Feminine Images of God from the Bible to the Early Kabbalah* (Princeton, NJ: Princeton University Press, 2002), 39–57. See also idem, *The Jewish Jesus: How Judaism and Christianity Shaped Each Other* (Princeton, NJ: Princeton University Press, 2012), 174ff.

2. Quod Deus immutabilis sit, §§31–32; De confusione linguarum, §§146–47.

3. On the interplay, see Schäfer, *Mirror of His Beauty*, 41–42.

4. De opificio mundi, §24. See also De fuga et inventione, §§12–13. The English translation follows Philo, "On the Creation of the World," in *Philo*, trans. F. H. Colson and G. H. Whitaker (Cambridge, MA: Loeb Classical Library, 1929), 1:21.

5. In Philo, according to Martin Hengel, "Jewish wisdom speculation is connected with the Platonic doctrine of creation found in the Timaeus." Martin Hengel, *The Son of God: The Origin of Christology and the History of Jewish Hellenistic Religion*, trans. John Bowden (1976; repr., Eugene, OR: Wipf and Stock, 2007), 51–52.

6. De confusione linguarum, §146. The English translation follows Philo, "On the Confusion of Tongues," in *Philo*, trans. F. H. Colson and G. H. Whitaker (Cambridge, MA: Loeb Classical Library, 1931), 4:89, 91.

7. De confusione linguarum, §147. The English translation follows ibidem, 91.

8. Quaestiones in Genesim, 2:62. The English translation follows Philo, *Questions and Answers on Genesis*, trans. Ralph Marcus (Cambridge, MA: Loeb Classical Library, 1953), Supplement 1:150. See also Hengel, *The Son of God*, 52.

9. Refers to the Word (Logos), which in John is identified with Jesus; hence "he" instead of "it."

10. David Winston, *Logos and Mystical Theology in Philo of Alexandria* (Cincinnati: Hebrew Union College Press, 1985), 10; David T. Runia, *Philo and the Church Fathers: A Collection of Papers* (Leiden: Brill, 1995).

Transition: From Pre-Christian to Post-Christian Judaism

1. The circle around Gabriele Boccaccini. See Boccaccini's short research report in his article "The Rediscovery of Enochic Judaism and the Enoch Seminar," in *The Origins of Enochic Judaism*, ed. Gabriele Boccaccini (Turin: Zamorani, 2002), 9–13. And see also the articles in this volume.

2. For the most important representatives, see Daniel Boyarin, "Once Again: 'Two Dominions in Heaven' in the Mekhilta," *Tarbiz* 81 (2012–13): 87–101 (Hebr.); idem, "Is Metatron a Converted Christian?" *Judaïsme Ancien / Ancient Judaism* 1 (2013): 13–62; Menahem Kister, "The Manifestations of God in the Midrashic Literature in Light of Christian Texts," *Tarbiz* 81 (2012–13): 103–42 (Hebr.); idem, "Metatron, God, and the 'Two Powers': The Dynamics of Tradition, Exegesis, and Polemic," *Tarbiz* 82 (2013–14): 43–88 (Hebr.).

Chapter 9: The Son of Man in the Midrash

1. With slight variations, the midrash is preserved at two different places in the Mekhilta, namely in *Mekhilta de-Rabbi Ishmael*, ba-hodesh 5 and *shirata* 4. See H. S. Horovitz and I. A. Rabin, eds., *Mekhilta de-Rabbi Ishmael* (Frankfurt, 1931), 129–30, 219–20; and Jacob Z. Lauterbach, ed., *Mekhilta de-Rabbi Ishmael* (Philadelphia, 1933, ²2004), 1:188–89; 2:314–15. In one of my very first articles, I analyzed this midrash complex with its numerous parallels. See Peter Schäfer, "Israel und die Völker der Welt. Zur Auslegung von Mekhilta deRabbi Yishma'el, bahodesh Yitro 5," *FJB* 4 (1976): 32–62. Now see also Peter Schäfer, *Die Geburt des Judentums aus dem Geist des Christentums. Fünf Vorlesungen zur Entstehung des rabbinischen Judentums* (Tübingen: Mohr Siebeck, 2010), 65ff.; idem, *The Jewish Jesus: How Judaism and*

Christianity Shaped Each Other (Princeton, NJ: Princeton University Press, 2012), 55ff; see also the respective contributions by Boyarin and above all Kister's article in *Tarbiz* 81.

2. "I am he who was at Sinai" only in the printed editions.

3. Or "I am he."

4. Schäfer, *Die Geburt des Judentums*, 69–70; idem, *The Jewish Jesus*, 59–60.

5. Daniel Boyarin, "Is Metatron a Converted Christian?," *Judaïsme Ancien / Ancient Judaism* 1 (2013): 28.

6. Final redaction around the seventh century CE, but the text contains numerous older traditions.

7. Died 1105.

8. Boyarin, "Metatron," 29ff.

9. Adiel Schremer, "Midrash, Theology, and History: Two Powers in Heaven Revisited," *JSJ* 39 (2008): 246.

10. Boyarin, "Metatron," 31.

11. Schäfer, *Die Geburt des Judentums*, 71; idem, *The Jewish Jesus*, 61. It gratifies me to see that such an experienced midrash exegete as Menahem Kister advocates a similar view (Kister, "Manifestations," 111f.): "I think the interpretations that were being attached to the quotation of this verse [Dan. 7:10] are dubious; it is possible that this verse is nothing but the continuation of the quotation of v. 9."

12. Boyarin, "Metatron," 32n37.

13. Boyarin ("Metatron," 36–37) takes offense that I am supposedly using a double standard: Whereas I reject Boyarin's Son of Man interpretation in the Mekhilta, because Daniel 7:13 is not explicitly quoted, I generously relate Aqiva's midrash in b Sanhedrin 38b to the Son of Man, although the verse Daniel 7:13 is also not cited there. Here he overlooks that the Talmud midrash is about David, and that for precisely that reason (the messiah-king David is the Son of Man), an explicit reference to Daniel 7:13 is not necessary. On Aqiva's midrash, see the next chapter.

14. On the direct parallels, see Kister, "Manifestations," 112ff.

15. Pesiqta Rabbati 21, ed. Meir Friedmann, *Pesiqta Rabbati* (Vienna, 1880), fol. 100b–101a. The English translation follows William G. Braude, *Pesikta Rabbati: Discourses for Feasts, Fasts, and Special Sabbaths* (New Haven, CT: Yale University Press, 1968), 1:421ff.

16. Kister, "Manifestations," 113 with note 52.

17. Presumably Hiyya II bar Abba, a contemporary of Rabbi Levi (early fourth century CE).

18. On the whore's son as an allusion to Jesus, see Peter Schäfer, *Jesus in the Talmud* (Princeton, NJ: Princeton University Press, 2007), 111–12.

19. See Schäfer, *Die Geburt des Judentums*, 33ff.; idem, *The Jewish Jesus*, 21ff.

20. Numerous midrashim go yet a step further and prove that even God's name *Elohim* usually collocates with a singular verb. See Schäfer, *Die Geburt des Judentums*, 37ff.; idem, *The Jewish Jesus*, 25–26.

21. Kister ("Manifestations") adds another perspective to the debate: it may well be that the different "appearances" of God in the Mekhilta and other midrashim do not aim as it were at ontologically different manifestations of God (and thus binitarian ideas), but in fact at how God is perceived from the perspective of Israel. In that case, the appearances of God would be phenomena in the eye of the beholder (Israel), yet not different modes of being of God. This is a noteworthy approach, which, however, cannot be discussed here.

22. Boyarin, "Metatron," 54, 21.

23. See Schäfer, *The Origins of Jewish Mysticism*, 10–11.

24. This is connected with endeavors to draw close ties between early Jewish apocalypticism (in particular the ascent accounts) and above all the Qumran literature and the emergence of early Jewish mysticism. For a book that especially propagates this idea, see Rachel Elior, *The Three Temples: On the Emergence of Jewish Mysticism* (Oxford: Littmann Library of Jewish Civilization, 2004). On this, see Schäfer, *The Origins of Jewish Mysticism*, 14ff.

25. The beginning of the Islamic period in Palestine in the early seventh century CE brought with it a renaissance of apocalyptic literature, especially the Apocalypse of Zerubbavel. See Peter Schäfer, *Mirror of His Beauty: Feminine Images of God from the Bible to the Early Kabbalah* (Princeton, NJ: Princeton University Press, 2002), 212ff.

26. The classic example in the Bavli also used by Boyarin ("Metatron," 57) is the elaborated small treatise on the seven heavens along with the associated cosmological and meteorological traditions that precede the Metatron discussion in the Bavli (b Hagigah 12b–13a). Some motifs are in fact taken up here that we know from the apocrypha and pseudepigrapha too, but they are hardly particularly significant, and above all, b Hagigah 12b–13a is the sole example for such an adaptation of apocalyptic traditions in the Bavli. It virtually goes without saying that they are radically reinterpreted in the Bavli. See Peter Schäfer, "From Cosmology to Theology: The Rabbinic Appropriation of Apocalyptic Cosmology," in *Creation and Re-Creation in Jewish Thought: Festschrift in Honor of Joseph Dan on the Occasion of His Seventieth Birthday*, ed. Rachel Elior and Peter Schäfer (Tübingen: Mohr Siebeck, 2005), 39–58.

27. Schäfer, *The Origins of Jewish Mysticism*, 323–24; idem, *Die Geburt des Judentums*, 129ff.; idem, *The Jewish Jesus*, 143.

28. Boyarin, "Metatron," 54ff.

29. In my review of Boyarin's *The Jewish Gospels*, I briefly outlined them for the first time, and it is the specific purpose of the present book to expand on them more precisely.

30. Boyarin, "Metatron," 14–15.

Chapter 10: The Son of Man–Messiah David

1. On the parallel b Sanhedrin 38b, see pp. 87ff. below.

2. The parallel in b Sanhedrin inserts here, "For it has been taught (in another baraita)."

3. On this in detail, see Menahem Kister, "Metatron, God, and the 'Two Powers': The Dynamics of Tradition, Exegesis, and Polemic," *Tarbiz* 82 (2013–14): 43–88 (Hebr.). The Munich Talmud manuscript Cod. Hebr. 6 has recorded only the two "bare" baraitot, without the artful structure of the Bavli redactor. According to Kister, they are tannaitic—that is, pre-Talmudic—but this is by no means necessarily the case. See Kister, "Metatron," 53, 53n56 (Hebr.).

4. Peter Schäfer, *Die Geburt des Judentums aus dem Geist des Christentums. Fünf Vorlesungen zur Entstehung des rabbinischen Judentums* (Tübingen: Mohr Siebeck, 2010), 79ff.; idem, *The Jewish Jesus: How Judaism and Christianity Shaped Each Other* (Princeton, NJ: Princeton University Press, 2012), 68ff.

5. Aqiva lived in the first half of the second century CE.

6. Mark 14:62. See also Matt. 26:64; Luke 22:69.

7. Boyarin does not want to rule out that the baraita could be an earlier and thus Palestinian source. He bases this on the tension in the text, according to which the anonymous voice of the Bavli first accepts the position that is then rejected in the cited baraita (the two thrones for God and David). I consider this an overly logical interpretation since the dialectic artfulness of the sugya lies precisely in first taking up Aqiva's position only then to reject it with exactly the same baraita from which it is taken. Daniel Boyarin, "Is Metatron a Converted Christian?" *Judaïsme Ancien / Ancient Judaism* 1 (2013): 23.

8. y Taanit 4:8/27, fol. 68d. See Peter Schäfer, *Der Bar Kokhba-Aufstand. Studien zum zweiten jüdischen Krieg gegen Rom* (Tübingen: Mohr Siebeck, 1981), 137ff.

9. Schäfer, *Die Geburt des Judentums*, 94f.; idem, *The Jewish Jesus*, 82.

10. Schäfer, ibidem.

11. Regardless of Boyarin's efforts to document them in the Mekhilta midrash discussed above. Boyarin ("Metatron," 26ff.) explicitly creates the connection between the Babylonian baraita and the Palestinian midrash in the Mekhilta: the Mekhilta is the express (and only) bridge between the pre-Christian binitarian traditions and the Bavli.

12. On this in detail, see Schäfer, *Die Geburt des Judentums*, 33ff.; idem, *The Jewish Jesus*, 27ff.

13. Plural in Hebrew.

14. Plural in Hebrew.

15. The angels.

16. "Watchers" and "holy ones" are also terms for the angels.

17. b Sanhedrin 38b. This is followed by the discussion in the baraita, as above in b Hagigah 14a.

18. On this in detail, see Anna Maria Schwemer, "Irdischer und himmlischer König. Beobachtungen zur sogenannten David-Apokalypse in Hekhalot Rabbati §§122–126," in *Königsherrschaft Gottes und himmlischer Kult im Judentum, Urchristentum und in der hellenistischen Welt*, ed. Martin Hengel and Anna Maria Schwemer (Tübingen: Mohr Siebeck, 1991), 309–59; Ulrike Hirschfelder, "The Liturgy of the Messiah: The Apocalypse of David in Hekhalot Literature," *JSQ* 12 (2005): 148–93.

19. Schwemer, "Irdischer und himmlischer König," 32.

20. Schäfer, *The Jewish Jesus*, 85–94.

21. Peter Schäfer, Margarete Schlüter, and Hans Georg von Mutius, *Synopse zur Hekhalot-Literatur* (Tübingen: Mohr Siebeck, 1981), §§125f.; Hirschfelder, "The Liturgy of the Messiah," 188ff. Translation based on Schäfer, *The Jewish Jesus*, 86–87.

22. "I," as in most manuscripts, instead of "he."

23. Literally run (*ratzin/ratzim*).

24. Although necessary to make sense, this is missing in almost all manuscripts with the exception of MSS New York 8128 and 3021.

25. As in all manuscripts with the exception of MS New York 8128: "toward my beloved one."

26. Numerous manuscripts add "and the holy creatures." Ofannim and Serafim are different classes of angels.

27. MS Budapest 238: "approached"; MS Leipzig 613: "shuddered"; MS New York 8128 (although this makes no sense): "were made."

28. Some manuscripts cite Exodus 15:18: "The Lord will reign forever and ever."

29. In two manuscripts, "angels."

30. In the sense of "special"; in some manuscripts, "praiseworthy."

31. In some manuscripts, "in the (great) Temple."

32. In some manuscripts, "four hundred."

33. This continuation only in some manuscripts.

34. In two manuscripts, "and all heavenly bodies."

35. And more often, for example, Ps. 96:10, Ps. 97:1.

36. I first developed this thesis rudimentarily in *The Jewish Jesus*, 85ff. Kister ("Metatron," 56n69) rejects it vehemently, going into detail on some minor details, but without engaging in the main point.

37. The Qedushah is a prayer in the synagogue service that revolves around the Trisagion ("Holy, holy, holy") of Isaiah 6:3.

38. Kister's ("Metatron," 56n69) long note is clearly an attempt to comply with the adage, "That which must not, cannot be." Hirschfelder offers a different take on this: "Although God here is expressly the subject of the Psalm verse, the context of

the ensuing royal procession definitely places the emphasis on David's celestial reign." Hirschfelder, "The Liturgy of the Messiah," 173.

39. The similarity between *dodi* (דודי) and *dawid* (דוד) is much more obvious in Hebrew.

40. Kister, "Metatron," ibidem; Hirschfelder, "The Liturgy of the Messiah," 189. Also, one must add, the New York manuscript is a late manuscript influenced by the *haside ashkenaz*.

41. See, for example, the variant reading "in the (great) Temple" (above, n. 31, below, n. 46).

42. Hirschfelder, "The Liturgy of the Messiah," 172; Schäfer, *The Jewish Jesus*, 89.

43. The *Shi'ur Qomah* texts describe and calculate the infinite dimensions of God's body from head to toe. Although God's body cannot be measured in earthly dimensions, the authors paradoxically do just that: they measure the length of the individual limbs of the divine body, although in immeasurable, fantastic numbers. On this genre of Hekhalot literature, see Christoph Markschies, *Gottes Körper. Jüdische, christliche und pagane Gottesvorstellungen in der Antike* (Munich: Beck, 2016), 202ff.

44. Hirschfelder, "The Liturgy of the Messiah," 172 with note 87.

45. Hirschfelder, ibidem, 172 with note 88.

46. Despite Kister's ("Metatron," 56n69) unconvincing objections, in view of the context, I prefer this reading over that of the "great house of learning."

47. Of course it is possible once again to object, as does Kister, that "opposite" does not mean "next to one another," and that "opposite" can also be translated as "corresponding."

48. Schäfer, Schlüter, and von Mutius, *Synopse zur Hekhalot-Literatur*, §295 in MS Budapest 238 (as an addition to the Sar ha-Torah complex) and §405 in MS New York 8121.

49. Because Psalm 146:10 is doubled, it makes sense to cite the parallel Exodus 15:18 for David.

50. Hirschfelder ("The Liturgy of the Messiah," 173, 178) clearly recognizes the special position of David in the Apocalypse, but in the end prefers to view the Messiah-King David as a substitute for the Merkavah mystic: no longer does the *yored merkavah* take the position of the Messiah, but the Messiah takes the position of the *yored merkavah*.

51. With this I am refining my deliberations in *The Jewish Jesus*, 91f. Kister ("Metatron," 56n69) dismisses them with the remark that I neglected to indicate that the cited Bible verses (including Zech. 14:9) are part of the Qedushah.

52. On this in greater detail, see Peter Schäfer, *The Origins of Jewish Mysticism* (Princeton, NJ: Princeton University Press, 2011), 103ff.; idem, *The Jewish Jesus*, 92ff.

53. Schäfer, *The Jewish Jesus*, 94.

54. Kister ("Metatron," 57–59) was the first to mention this.

55. *Contra Haereses* 32:1. Ephrem the Syrian, "Hymnen gegen die Irrlehren (Hymni contra haereses)," in *Des heiligen Ephräm des Syrers ausgewählte Schriften*, trans. from Syrian and Greek, vol. 1. *Bibliothek der Kirchenväter*, series 1, vol. 61 (Munich: J. Kösel & F. Pustet, 1928).

56. Daniel 7:13.

57. Daniel 7:9.

58. Daniel 7:10.

59. *Contra Haereses* 32:5–6.

60. Christoph Markschies, *Alta Trinità Beata* (Tübingen: Mohr Siebeck, 2000), 13ff. Kister ("Metatron," 57n74) correctly notes that the Syriac *bar motva* corresponds to the Greek *synthronos*.

61. Johannes Chrysostomus, *Contra Anomoeos* 11 (Migne, PG 48, 800). See Jean Chrysostome, *Sur l'égalité du Père et du Fils. Contre les Anoméens homélies VII–XII*, in *Sources Chrétiennes*, trans. Anne-Marie Malingrey (Paris: Cerf, 1994), 304f.

62. Kister, "Metatron," 58.

Chapter 11: From the Human Enoch to the Lesser God Metatron

1. On this in greater detail, see Peter Schäfer, *Anziehung und Abstoßung. Juden und Christen in den ersten Jahrhunderten ihrer Begegnung / Attraction and Repulsion: Jews and Christians in the First Centuries of Their Encounter*, bilingual ed. (Tübingen: Mohr Siebeck, 2015); idem, "*Genesis Rabbah's Enoch*," in *Genesis Rabbah in Text and Context*, ed. Sarit Kattan Gribetz, David M. Grossberg, Martha Himmelfarb, and Peter Schäfer (Tübingen: Mohr Siebeck: 2016), 63–80.

2. 1 Enoch 12–16.

3. Philip R. Davies, "And Enoch Was Not, for Genesis Took Him," in *Biblical Traditions in Transmission: Essays in Honour of Michael A. Knibb*, ed. Charlotte Hempel and Judith M. Lieu (Leiden: Brill, 2006), 97–107.

4. 2 Enoch 22:8–10. See Peter Schäfer, *The Origins of Jewish Mysticism* (Princeton, NJ: Princeton University Press, 2011), 77ff.

5. See Peter Schäfer, "Metatron in Babylonia," in *Hekhalot Literature in Context: Between Byzantium and Babylonia*, ed. Ra'anan Boustan, Martha Himmelfarb, and Peter Schäfer (Tübingen: Mohr Siebeck, 2013), 29–39. Klaus Herrmann vehemently argues for a Byzantine cultural background of the earliest layers of 3 Enoch (whichever these might be), but the supposed "absorption of visual impressions"—with that he means Byzantine iconography—is not much more than an impression gained from the splendid mosaics of Ravenna, and certainly no easier to prove than the

conflict I postulate between the Metatron ideology of 3 Enoch and New Testament Christology (the "literary dependency" demanded for the latter is in any case a chimera). Moreover, the clear-cut distinction between "Byzantine" and "Babylonian-Sasanian" cultural spheres seems to me far too static, and thus not very helpful. See Klaus Herrmann, "Jewish Mysticism in Byzantium: The Transformation of Merkavah Mysticism in 3 Enoch," in ibidem, 85n1, 107.

6. Genesis Rabbah 25:1.

7. The other verse that mentions Enoch is the Epistle of Jude 1:14, which cites the pseudepigraphic Book of Enoch (1:9).

8. Set in quotation marks in the cited passage.

9. Justin Martyr, Dialogue with Trypho, 19:3.

10. Clemens Alexandrinus, Stromata, IV, 17:3; ibid., II, 15:3.

11. Irenaeus, Adversus Haereses, IV, 16:2. See also ibidem V, 5:1.

12. Tertullian, Adversus Iudaeos, 2:13. See also ibidem, chap. 4.

13. Tertullian, De resurrectione mortuorum, 58:9.

14. Tertullian, De anima, 50.

15. y Taan 2:1/24, fol. 65b; Exodus Rabbah 29:5. See Peter Schäfer, *Jesus in the Talmud* (Princeton, NJ: Princeton University Press, 2007), 107–9.

16. A notable exception are the Targumim, the Aramaic translations of the Pentateuch. See Schäfer, "*Genesis Rabbah's* Enoch," 78–80.

17. This is an allusion to Elijah's ascent to heaven (2 Kings 2:11).

18. Peter Schäfer, Margaret Schlüter, and Hans Georg von Mutius, *Synopse zur Hekhalot-Literatur* (Tübingen: Mohr Siebeck, 1981), §9.

19. Schäfer, Schlüter, and von Mutius, ibid., §11. The English translations are based on Philip S. Alexander, "3 Enoch," in *The Old Testament Pseudepigrapha*, ed. James H. Charlesworth (New York: Doubleday, 1983), §8:2, 1:263.

20. More precisely, according to the dimensions of the "world in length and breadth"; that is, he made him as big as the earthly world.

21. Schäfer, Schlüter, and von Mutius, ibid., §12; Alexander, "3 Enoch," §9:4, 1:263.

22. Schäfer, Schlüter, and von Mutius, ibid., §13; Alexander, "3 Enoch," §10:2, 1:264.

23. Schäfer, Schlüter, and von Mutius, ibid., §13; Alexander, "3 Enoch," §10:3, 1:264.

24. Schäfer, Schlüter, and von Mutius, ibid., §13; Alexander, "3 Enoch," §10:4–5, 1:264.

25. Schäfer, Schlüter, and von Mutius, ibid., §14; Alexander, "3 Enoch," §11:2–3, 1:264.

26. The number forty-nine is evidently taken from the rabbinic literature: Moses received forty-nine of the fifty gates of understanding that were created in the world

(b Nedarim 38a), and at the end of days, the light of the sun will be forty-nine times brighter than it is now (Exodus Rabbah 15:21).

27. Schäfer, Schlüter, and von Mutius, *Synopse zur Hekhalot-Literatur*, §15; Alexander, "3 Enoch," §12:3–5, 1:265.

28. The spelling of God's name varies in the manuscripts.

29. Literally "within him."

30. Schäfer, Schlüter, and von Mutius, *Synopse zur Hekhalot-Literatur*, §16; Alexander, "3 Enoch," §13:1, 1:265–66.

31. Schäfer, Schlüter, and von Mutius, ibid., §§17–18; Alexander, "3 Enoch," §14:5, 1:267.

32. Schäfer, Schlüter, and von Mutius, ibid., §19; Alexander, "3 Enoch," §15, 1:267.

33. Schäfer, Schlüter, and von Mutius, ibid., §20; Alexander, "3 Enoch," §16:1, 1:268.

34. Schäfer, Schlüter, and von Mutius, ibid., §20; Alexander, "3 Enoch," §16:2–5, 1:268.

35. From the boundless secondary literature on the two versions of the episode in 3 Enoch and the Talmud, I mention here only the (presently) two most recent contributions that deal extensively with their predecessors: Daniel Boyarin, "Is Metatron a Converted Christian?" *Judaïsme Ancien / Ancient Judaism* 1 (2013): 13–62; David M. Grossberg, "Between 3 Enoch and Bavli *Hagigah*: Heresiology and Orthopraxy in the Ascent of Elisha ben Avuyah," in *Hekhalot Literature in Context: Between Byzantium and Babylonia*, ed. Ra'anan Boustan, Martha Himmelfarb, and Peter Schäfer (Tübingen: Mohr Siebeck, 2013), 117–39.

36. Boyarin misjudges the editorial context in 3 Enoch, when following Alexander he claims "that the purpose of the author of 3 Enoch was to validate Metatron speculation." Daniel Boyarin, "Beyond Judaisms: Metatron and the Divine Polymorphy of Ancient Judaism," *JSJ* 41 (2010): 349; idem, "Metatron," 45.

37. In contrast to the beginning of the section, this passage does not specifically reassert that Metatron is sitting at the *entrance* to the palace/heaven—as distinct from God, who is enthroned in its midst.

38. In Greek, this is expressed as *exousia* and *dynamis*; on this in greater detail, see Alan F. Segal, *Two Powers in Heaven: Early Rabbinic Reports about Christianity and Gnosticism* (Leiden: Brill, 1977), 7–8n8.

39. This is also correctly mentioned in Boyarin, "Metatron," 46–47.

40. On punishments with lashes of light or fire, see also b Yoma 77a (Gabriel) and b Bava Metzia 47a.

41. b Hagiga 15a. Here I am further developing the observations introduced in Peter Schäfer, *Die Geburt des Judentums aus dem Geist des Christentums. Fünf Vorlesungen zur Entstehung des rabbinischen Judentums* (Tübingen: Mohr Siebeck, 2010),

114ff.; idem, *The Jewish Jesus: How Judaism and Christianity Shaped Each Other* (Princeton, NJ: Princeton University Press, 2012), 127ff.

42. On the development of this narrative, see Schäfer, *The Origins of Jewish Mysticism*, 196ff.

43. For the most comprehensive analysis with all text variations, see Menahem Kister, "Metatron, God, and the 'Two Powers': The Dynamics of Tradition, Exegesis, and Polemic," *Tarbiz* 82 (2013–14): 63ff. (Hebr.).

44. "To sit down" or "to be seated" is missing in the otherwise important manuscript Munich 95, but this is obviously a scribal error, or more specifically a haplography (omission in writing of one of two adjacent and similar words)—in this case, *lemetav* (to sit) and *lemikhtav* (to write).

45. "No standing" in most manuscripts. See David Halperin, *The Merkabah in Rabbinic Literature* (New Haven, CT: American Oriental Society, 1980), 167 with note 84.

46. "No jealousy" (*qin'ah*) in most manuscripts. See Halperin, *The Merkabah in Rabbinic Literature*, ibid. with note 88.

47. On this in detail, see Kister, "Metatron," 65ff. Kister (68) introduces the subtle difference between "text-based truth" and "tradition-based truth": the text must be accepted as it is and may not be carelessly emended. Nevertheless, the *message* of the text can stand in contrast to the traditional wording. As much as I agree with Kister in the matter itself, this distinction is dangerous because it can of course be easily misused.

48. For example, in Boyarin, "Metatron," 41ff.

49. I disagree here with Boyarin ("Metatron," 41–42), who wrongly criticizes Alexander: "His [Alexander's] interpretation of the conflict or competition as between different angels and not as rivalry with God quite misses the point in my opinion (41n58)."

50. It is no longer possible to reconstruct how the "*no* standing" came to be included in the original tradition.

51. According to Ezekiel 1:7, the legs of the four creatures that carry God's throne are straight; that is, they have no knee joints. See Genesis Rabbah 65:21, where an interpretation from Daniel 7:16 is added.

52. See H. S. Horovitz, ed., *Sifre Numeri*, §42, 47; M. Higger, ed., *Tractate Derekh Eretz*, chap. 8, 120. *Pace* Boyarin ("Metatron," 42n61), the absence of jealousy has nothing to do with the fact that God is a jealous God, and that in this respect too, the angels are distinct from God.

53. This is obviously also derived from Ezekiel (1:9), where it is said of the four creatures that they do not turn as they move, always moving straight ahead in the direction of their faces. See also Genesis Rabbah 49:7. The back has nothing to do with God's back in Exodus 33:23 (*pace* Boyarin, "Metatron," 42).

54. Because they are not mortal as humans are, and not because God had to rest on the seventh day (Boyarin, "Metatron," 42n61). Kister ("Metatron," 66n120) refers to the parallel *Tractate Derekh Eretz* (292–93), where the inability of the angels to procreate (Hebr. *ribbui*) is also mentioned—one of the possible meanings of the root *'pp* in Syriac. I find this, however, far-fetched.

55. Triggered especially by the seminal article by Philip S. Alexander, "3 Enoch and the Talmud," *JSJ* 18 (1987): 54ff. The most recent comprehensive contribution (up to now) is Boyarin, "Metatron," 44ff.

56. See also Kister, "Metatron," 60–61 with note 90.

57. As expressly mentioned also in Kister, "Metatron," 69–70.

58. Grossberg, "Between 3 Enoch and Bavli *Hagigah*."

59. Grossberg correctly notes that only at the very end of the narrative—namely, when encountering the prostitute—is Elisha referred to as "Aher."

60. b Bava Metzia 59h.

61. Schäfer, Schlüter, and von Mutius, *Synopse zur Hekhalot-Literatur*, §597 (only in MSS Oxford 1531 and New York 8128; the translation follows MS Oxford). In the following, I summarize my observations presented in *The Jewish Jesus*, 131–38.

62. Literally, "paradise"; here this refers to the highest of the seven heavens or palaces.

63. Literally, "with which the humans compare."

64. From the root *katar* (to crown) or *keter* (crown), apparently meaning the angel who is crowned.

65. This is also stated in Kister, "Metatron," 61. Yet Kister then reads the message of the 3 Enoch and Bavli version into this text.

66. "Unexpected" against the background of the 3 Enoch and Bavli version.

67. Kister, "Metatron," 61n93.

68. Ibidem.

69. The tenor of his argument is a case of *Roma locuta, causa finita* (Rome has spoken, the case is closed), as is unfortunately often the case with Kister's remarks.

70. b Berakhot 7a.

71. This means: that I do not go to the extreme and follow the law strictly.

72. Second generation of the Babylonian Amoraim and a student of Rav.

73. The Hebrew word *barakh* ("bless" and "praise") means here more specifically "recite a blessing" in the sense of composing a prayer.

74. As expressed also in Kister, "Metatron," 61n94.

75. The fact that both here and in "The Mysteries of Sandelfon" Akatriel carries the epithet *YH* (a form of the tetragrammaton *YHWH*) is not significant, as particularly high angels in the Hekhalot literature also carry this epithet.

76. b Sanhedrin 38b. For a discussion of this text, see Schäfer, *Die Geburt des Judentums*, 97ff.; idem, *The Jewish Jesus*, 104ff. Here I will again limit myself to the

most significant points and a discussion of the secondary literature that has since been published. For the most comprehensive analysis to date, see Kister, "Metatron," 75ff.

77. And not, as Lazarus Goldschmidt [*Der Babylonische Talmud*, vol. 8, *Baba Bathra / Synhedrin* (repr., Berlin: Jüdischer Verlag, 1967), 611] and others suggest, "This said Metatron," in the sense of "And unto Moses he [Metatron] said: Come up to the Lord (*YHWH*)." This is improbable both linguistically and in terms of subject matter: *zehu Metatron* means "this is Metatron" and not "this said Metatron," and as regards our subject, it is precisely the identity of their names (God and Metatron have the same name) that is the key here.

78. Literally, "do not exchange me for him."

79. *Parwanqa* is a Persian loanword, derived from the Middle Iranian *parwānak* (Middle Persian *parwānag*); it means "guide, messenger, precursor." See Michael Sokoloff, *A Dictionary of Jewish Babylonian Aramaic of the Talmudic and Geonic Periods* (Ramat-Gan: Bar Ilan University Press; Baltimore: Johns Hopkins University Press, 2002), 929.

80. Literally, "if your face goes not."

81. b Sanhedrin 38b. See Schäfer, *The Jewish Jesus*, 38.

82. Justin Martyr, *Dialogue with Trypho*, 56:23; see also 60:2.

83. Or, "do not defy him!"

84. This is also the interpretation of Exodus 33:14–15 in the Septuagint, which translates the "face" (see above, n. 80) unequivocally with *autos* (you yourself).

85. From the context, this clearly refers to God.

86. Despite Joseph Dan's attempts to confirm this. Joseph Dan, *The Ancient Jewish Mysticism* (Tel Aviv: MOD Books, 1993), 109–10.

87. Apocalypse of Abraham 10:3 and 8. R. Rubinkiewicz, "Apocalypse of Abraham," in *The Old Testament Pseudepigrapha*, ed. James H. Charlesworth (New York: Doubleday, 1983), 1:693–94.

88. Iao/Iaho is the Greek form of the Hebrew *YHWH*.

89. Peter Schäfer and Klaus Herrmann, *Übersetzung der Hekhalot-Literatur* (Tübingen: Mohr Siebeck, 1995), 1:lii. On this in detail, see Kister, "Metatron," 76.

90. As early as Philo (*De Agricultura*, 51), the angel in Exodus 23:20 is interpreted as the "Logos and firstborn son," which of course opened the door to Christological speculations.

91. Kister, "Metatron," 84ff.

92. Peter Schäfer, *Geniza-Fragmente zur Hekhalot-Literatur* (Tübingen: Mohr Siebeck, 1984), 132 (T.-S. K 21:95.J, fol. 1a, lines 1–17).

93. Kister ("Metatron," 80n219) correctly indicates that *eresh* is not a miswritten form of *ro'sh*, as I had erroneously assumed, but instead common in liturgical poetry (*piyyut*), meaning something like "speech." More appropriate here is perhaps

"meditation, devotion." See Marcus Jastrow, *A Dictionary of the Targumim, the Talmud Babli and Yerushalmi, and the Midrashic Literature* (New York: Pardes, 1950), 1:126.

94. Literally, "Beware of his face," that is, of him.

95. The following line of text is indented here—that is, the scribe wanted to indicate a break in the text.

96. Literally, "he is mistaken."

97. Schäfer, *Geniza-Fragmente*, 131.

98. Kister ("Metatron," 39) correctly refers to it as "bold."

99. Schäfer, *Geniza-Fragmente*, 176–79 (T.-S. K 21.95.A, fol. 2a, line 22 to fol. 2b, line 2).

100. Followed by explanations of the three names.

101. In the sense of "from this point of reference."

102. The text is to be corrected as *"yelekh,"* as in Kister, "Metatron," 84.

103. As is common, the tetragrammaton YHWH is rendered here as "the Lord," though more precisely "the Lord God" is meant.

104. There is a gap in the text. The missing word could be *mal'akh* (angel).

105. Schäfer, *Geniza-Fragmente*, 171.

106. Literally, perhaps something like "arguing/deciding/interceding spirit." Apart from the Hekhalot literature, it is mentioned only in the Babylonian Talmud. See b Sanhedrin 44b, where he argues with God.

107. Schäfer and Herrmann, *Übersetzung der Hekhalot-Literatur*, vol. 1, §76.

108. The reference to Job 1:7 (see Schäfer, *Geniza-Fragmente*, 180, on fol. 2a/28) is correct, but in our context this can only be referring to Zechariah 3:2, as Kister ("Metatron," 84f.) correctly recognized.

109. Of course, only a fool would propose that the attribution of these verses to Rabbi Yehoshua was influenced by the High Priest Yehoshua.

110. This is also the case in the unified German translation, which renders the verse as follows, without any additional commentary: "The angel of the Lord said to Satan."

111. See above, p. 116.

112. Kister, "Metatron," 82ff.

113. And it sometimes even contradicts Kister's own (astute and correct) analysis.

BIBLIOGRAPHY

Ahn, Gregor. "Monotheismus und Polytheismus I: Religionswissenschaftlich." In *RGG*, edited by Hans Dieter Betz, Don S. Browning, Bernd Janowski, and Eberhard Jüngel, vol. 5, cols. 1457–59. Tübingen: Mohr Siebeck, ⁴2002.

Alexander, Philip S. "3 Enoch." In *The Old Testament Pseudepigrapha*, edited by James H. Charlesworth, 1:223–315. New York: Doubleday, 1983.

———. "3 Enoch and the Talmud." *JSJ* 18 (1987): 40–68.

———. " 'The Agent of the King Is Treated as the King Himself': Does the Worship of Jesus Imply His Divinity?" In *In the Fullness of Time: Essays on Christology, Creation, and Eschatology in Honor of Richard Bauckham*, edited by Daniel M. Gurtner, Grant Macaskill, and Jonathan T. Pennington, 97–114. Grand Rapids, MI: Eerdmans, 2016.

Anonymous. *The Palestinian Targum to the Pentateuch: Codex Vatican (Neofiti 1)*. Jerusalem: Makor, 1970.

Assmann, Jan. *Ma'at. Gerechtigkeit und Unsterblichkeit im Alten Ägypten*. Munich: Beck, 1990.

———. *Moses the Egyptian: The Memory of Egypt in Western Monotheism*. Cambridge, MA: Harvard University Press, 1997.

Baillet, Maurice. *Qumrân Grotte 4.3 (4Q482–4Q520)*. DJD 7. Oxford: Clarendon Press, 1982.

Barker, Margaret. *The Great Angel: A Study of Israel's Second God*. London: SPCK, 1992.

———. *The Great High Priest: The Temple Roots of Christian Liturgy*. London: T and T Clark, 2003.

Bauckham, Richard. *God Crucified: Monotheism and Christology in the New Testament*. Grand Rapids, MI: Eerdmans, 1998.

———. *Jesus and the God of Israel: God Crucified and Other Studies on the New Testament's Christology of Divine Identity*. Grand Rapids, MI: Eerdmans, 2008.

———. "Devotion to Jesus Christ in Earliest Christianity: An Appraisal and Discussion of the Work of Larry Hurtado." In *Mark, Manuscripts, and Monotheism:*

Essays in Honor of Larry W. Hurtado, edited by Chris Keith and Dieter T. Roth, 176–200. London: Bloomsbury, 2015.

Boccaccini, Gabriele. "The Rediscovery of Enochic Judaism and the Enoch Seminar." In *The Origins of Enochic Judaism,* edited by Gabriele Boccaccini, 9–13. Turin: Zamorani, 2002.

Boyarin, Daniel. "The Gospel of the Memra: Jewish Binitarianism and the Prologue to John." *HTR* 94 (2001): 243–84.

———. *Border Lines: The Partition of Judaeo-Christianity.* Philadelphia: University of Pennsylvania Press, 2004.

———. "Two Powers in Heaven; or, The Making of a Heresy." In *The Idea of Biblical Interpretation: Essays in Honor of James L. Kugel,* edited by Hindy Najman and Judith H. Newman, 331–70. Leiden: Brill, 2004.

———. "The Parables of Enoch and the Foundation of the Rabbinic Sect: A Hypothesis." In *"The Words of a Wise Man's Mouth Are Gracious" (Qoh 10,12): Festschrift for Günter Stemberger on the Occasion of His 65th Birthday,* edited by Mauro Perani, 53–72. Berlin: Walter de Gruyter, 2005.

———. "Beyond Judaisms: Meṭaṭron and the Divine Polymorphy of Ancient Judaism." *JSJ* 41 (2010): 323–65.

———. "Daniel 7, Intertextuality, and the History of Israel's Cult." *HTR* 105, no. 2 (2012): 139–62.

———. *The Jewish Gospels: The Story of the Jewish Christ.* New York: New Press, 2012.

———. "Once Again: 'Two Dominions in Heaven' in the Mekhilta." *Tarbiz* 81, (2012–13): 87–101 (Hebr.).

———. "Is Metatron a Converted Christian?" *Judaïsme Ancien / Ancient Judaism* 1 (2013): 13–62.

Chrysostom, John. *Sur l'égalité du Père et du Fils. Contre les Anoméens homélies VII–XII.* Sources Chrétiennes 396, translated by Anne-Marie Malingrey. Paris: Cerf, 1994.

Collins, Adela Yarbro, and John J. Collins. *King and Messiah as Son of God: Divine, Human, and Angelic Messianic Figures in Biblical and Related Literature.* Grand Rapids, MI: Eerdmans, 2008.

Collins, John J. *Daniel: A Commentary on the Book of Daniel.* Minneapolis: Fortress Press, 1993.

———. *The Scepter and the Star: The Messiahs of the Dead Sea Scrolls and Other Ancient Literature.* New York: Doubleday, 1995.

———. *The Scepter and the Star: Messianism in Light of the Dead Sea Scrolls.* Grand Rapids, MI: Eerdmans, ²2010.

Cross, Frank Moore. *Canaanite Myth and Hebrew Epic.* Cambridge, MA: Harvard University Press, 1973.

———. *The Ancient Library at Qumran.* Sheffield: Sheffield Academic Press, 1995.

———. "The Structure of the Apocalypse of 'Son of God' (4Q246)." In *Emanuel: Studies in Hebrew Bible, Septuagint, and Dead Sea Scrolls in Honor of Emanuel Tov,* edited by Shalom M. Paul, Robert A. Kraft, Lawrence H. Schiffman, and Weston W. Fields, 151–58. Leiden: Brill, 2003.

Dan, Joseph. *The Ancient Jewish Mysticism.* Tel Aviv: MOD Books, 1993.

Davies, Philip R. "And Enoch Was Not, for Genesis Took Him." In *Biblical Traditions in Transmission: Essays in Honour of Michael A. Knibb,* edited by Charlotte Hempel and Judith M. Lieu, 97–107. Leiden: Brill, 2006.

Díez Macho, Alejandro: *Neophyti 1: Targum Palestinense MS de la Biblioteca Vaticana.* Vol. 1, *Genesis: Edición Príncipe, Introducción General y Versión Castellana.* Madrid: Consejo Superior de Investigaciones Científicas, 1968.

Elior, Rachel. *The Three Temples: On the Emergence of Jewish Mysticism.* Oxford: Littmann Library of Jewish Civilization, 2004.

Emerton, John A. "The Origin of the Son of Man Imagery." *JTS* 9 (1958): 225–42.

Ephrem the Syrian. *Des heiligen Ephräm des Syrers ausgewählte Schriften.* Translated from Syrian and Greek. Vol. 1. *Bibliothek der Kirchenväter,* series 1, vol. 61. Munich: J. Kösel & F. Pustet, 1928.

Eshel, Esther. "4Q471B: A Self-Glorification Hymn." *RdQ* 17/65–68 (1996): 175–203.

Flusser, David. "The Hubris of the Antichrist in a Fragment from Qumran." *Immanuel* 10 (1980):31–37.

———. *Judaism and the Origins of Christianity.* Jerusalem: Magnes Press, 1998.

García Martínez, Florentino. "The Eschatological Figure of 4Q246." In *Qumran and Apocalyptic: Studies on the Aramaic Texts from Qumran,* 162–79. Leiden: Brill, 1992.

———. "Two Messianic Figures in the Qumran Texts." In *Current Research and Technological Developments on the Dead Sea Scrolls: Conference on the Texts from the Judean Desert, Jerusalem, 30 April, 1995,* edited by Donald W. Parry and Stephen D. Ricks, 14–40. Leiden: Brill, 1996.

García Martínez, Florentino, and Eibert J. C. Tigchelaar, eds. *The Dead Sea Scrolls Study Edition.* Leiden: Brill, 1997.

Goldschmidt, Lazarus. *Der Babylonische Talmud.* Vol. 8, *Baba Bathra / Synhedrin* (1st half). Reprint, Berlin: Jüdischer Verlag, 1967.

Grossberg, David M. "Between 3 Enoch and Bavli *Hagigah*: Heresiology and Orthopraxy in the Ascent of Elisha ben Abuyah." In *Hekhalot Literature in Context: Between Byzantium and Babylonia,* edited by Ra'anan Boustan, Martha Himmelfarb, and Peter Schäfer, 117–39. Tübingen: Mohr Siebeck 2013.

Halperin, David. *The Merkabah in Rabbinic Literature.* New Haven, CT: American Oriental Society, 1980.

Hayman, Peter. "Monotheism—A Misused Word in Jewish Studies?" *JJS* 42 (1991): 1–15.

Hengel, Martin. "Der Sohn Gottes." In *Studien zur Christologie. Kleine Schriften IV*, 74–145. Tübingen: Mohr Siebeck, 2006.

————. *The Son of God: The Origin of Christology and the History of Jewish Hellenistic Religion*. Translated by John Bowden. Reprint, Eugene, OR: Wipf and Stock, 2007. First published 1976 by Fortress Press.

Herford, R. Travers. *Christianity in Talmud and Midrash*. Expanded reprint, Jersey City, NJ: Ktav, 2006. First published 1903 by Williams and Norgate (London).

Herrmann, Klaus. "Jewish Mysticism in Byzantium: The Transformation of Merkavah Mysticism in 3 Enoch." In *Hekhalot Literature in Context: Between Byzantium and Babylonia*, edited by Ra'anan Boustan, Martha Himmelfarb, and Peter Schäfer, 85–116. Tübingen: Mohr Siebeck 2013.

Hirschfelder, Ulrike. "The Liturgy of the Messiah: The Apocalypse of David in Hekhalot Literature." *JSQ* 12 (2005): 148–93.

Hurtado, Larry W. *One God, One Lord: Early Christian Devotion and Ancient Jewish Monotheism*. London: SCM Press, 1988.

————. *How on Earth Did Jesus Become a God?: Historical Questions about Earliest Devotion to Jesus*. Grand Rapids, MI: Eerdmanns, 2005.

————. *God in New Testament Theology*. Nashville, TN: Abingdon, 2010.

————. "Richard Bauckham's Christological Pilgrimage." In *In the Fullness of Time: Essays on Christology, Creation, and Eschatology in Honor of Richard Bauckham*, edited by Daniel M. Gurtner, Grant Macaskill, and Jonathan T. Pennington, 82–96. Grand Rapids, MI: Eerdmans, 2016.

Idel, Moshe. *Ben: Sonship and Jewish Mysticism*. London: Continuum, 2007.

Jastrow, Marcus. *A Dictionary of the Targumim, the Talmud Babli and Yerushalmi, and the Midrashic Literature*. Vol. 1. New York: Pardes, 1950.

Kaiser, Otto, ed. *TUAT*. Vol. 2, *Religiöse Texte: Grab-, Sarg-, Votiv- und Bauinschriften*, edited by Christel Butterweck, Diethelm Conrad, Wilhelmus C. Feldman, Manfried Dietrich, Karl Hecker, Heike Sternberg-el Hotabi, Frank Kammerzell, Oswald Lorentz, Hans-Peter Müller, Walter W. Müller, Boyo Ockinga, Willem H. Ph. Römer, and Hans P. Roschinski. Gütersloh: Mohn, 1988.

Kautzsch, Emil. *Die Apokryphen und Pseudepigraphen des Alten Testaments*. Vol. 2, *Die Pseudepigraphen*. Tübingen: J.C.B. Mohr, 1900.

Kayatz, Christa. *Studien zu Proverbien 1–9. Eine form- und motivgeschichtliche Untersuchung unter Einbeziehung ägyptischen Vergleichsmaterials*. Neukirchen-Vluyn: Neukirchener Verlag, 1966.

Kister, Menachem. "The Manifestations of God in the Midrashic Literature in Light of Christian Texts." *Tarbiz* 81 (2012–13): 103–42 (Hebr.).

————. "Metatron, God, and the 'Two Powers': The Dynamics of Tradition, Exegesis, and Polemic." *Tarbiz* 82 (2013–14): 43–88 (Hebr.).

Klein, Michael L., ed. *The Fragment-Targums of the Pentateuch according to Their Extant Sources*. Vol. 1, *Text, Indices, and Introductory Essays*. Rome: Biblical Institute Press, 1980. Vol. 2, *Translations*. Rome: Biblical Institute Press, 1980.

Knohl, Israel. *The Messiah before Jesus: The Suffering Servant of the Dead Sea Scrolls*. Berkeley: University of California Press, 2000.

Lang, Bernhard. *Frau Weisheit. Deutung einer biblischen Gestalt*. Düsseldorf: Patmos, 1975.

Mack, Burton L. *Logos und Sophia. Untersuchungen zur Weisheitstheologie im hellenistischen Judentum*. Göttingen: Vandenhoeck and Ruprecht, 1973.

Maier, Johann. *Die Qumran-Essener. Die Texte vom Toten Meer*. Vol. 2. Munich: Ernst Reinhardt Verlag, 1995.

Markschies, Christoph. *Alta Trinità Beata*. Tübingen: Mohr Siebeck, 2000.

———. *Gottes Körper. Jüdische, christliche und pagane Gottesvorstellungen in der Antike*. Munich: Beck, 2016.

McNamara, Martin. *Targum Neofiti 1: Genesis*. The Aramaic Bible, Volume 1A. Collegeville, MN: Michael Glazier, 1992.

Metzger, B. M. "The Fourth Book of Ezra." In *The Old Testament Pseudepigrapha*, edited by James H. Charlesworth, 1:517–59. New York: Doubleday, 1983.

Milik, Józef T. "Milkî-ṣedek et Milkî-reša' dans les anciens écrits juifs et chrétiens." *JJS* 23 (1972): 95–144.

Müller, Hans-Peter. "Monotheismus und Polytheismus II: Altes Testament." In *RGG*, edited by Hans Dieter Betz, Don S. Browning, Bernd Janowski, and Eberhard Jüngel, vol. 5, cols. 1459–62. Tübingen: Mohr Siebeck, ⁴2002.

Nickelsburg, George W. E., and James C. VanderKam, eds. *1 Enoch: The Hermeneia Translation*. Minneapolis: Fortress Press, 2012.

Plöger, Otto. *Sprüche Salomos (Proverbia)*. Neukirchen-Vluyn: Neukirchener Verlag, 1984 (³2011).

Rubinkiewicz, R. "Apocalypse of Abraham." In *The Old Testament Pseudepigrapha*, edited by James H. Charlesworth, 1:680–705, New York: Doubleday, 1983.

Runia, David T. *Philo and the Church Fathers: A Collection of Papers*. Leiden: Brill, 1995.

Schäfer, Peter. "Israel und die Völker der Welt. Zur Auslegung von Mekhilta deRabbi Yishma'el, bahodesh Yitro 5." *FJB* 4 (1976): 32–62.

———. "Bibelübersetzungen II: Targumin." In *TRE*, edited by Gerhard Krause and Gerhard Müller, 6:216–28. Tübingen: Mohr Siebeck, 1980.

———. *Der Bar Kokhba-Aufstand. Studien zum zweiten jüdischen Krieg gegen Rom*. Tübingen: Mohr Siebeck, 1981.

———. *Geniza-Fragmente zur Hekhalot-Literatur*. Tübingen: Mohr Siebeck, 1984.

———. *Übersetzung der Hekhalot-Literatur*. Vol. 2: §§81–334. Tübingen: Mohr Siebeck, 1987.

————. *Mirror of His Beauty: Feminine Images of God from the Bible to the Early Kabbalah.* Princeton, NJ: Princeton University Press, 2002.

————. "From Cosmology to Theology: The Rabbinic Appropriation of Apocalyptic Cosmology." In *Creation and Re-Creation in Jewish Thought: Festschrift in Honor of Joseph Dan on the Occasion of His Seventieth Birthday*, edited by Rachel Elior and Peter Schäfer, 39–58. Tübingen: Mohr Siebeck, 2005.

————. *Jesus in the Talmud.* Princeton, NJ: Princeton University Press, 2007.

————. *Die Geburt des Judentums aus dem Geist des Christentums. Fünf Vorlesungen zur Entstehung des rabbinischen Judentums.* Tübingen: Mohr Siebeck, 2010.

————. *The Origins of Jewish Mysticism.* Princeton, NJ: Princeton University Press, 2011.

————. "The Jew Who Would Be God." *New Republic*, June 7, 2012, 36–39.

————. *The Jewish Jesus: How Judaism and Christianity Shaped Each Other.* Princeton, NJ: Princeton University Press, 2012.

————. "Metatron in Babylonia." In *Hekhalot Literature in Context: Between Byzantium and Babylonia*, edited by Ra'anan Boustan, Martha Himmelfarb, and Peter Schäfer, 29–39. Tübingen: Mohr Siebeck 2013.

————. *Anziehung und Abstoßung. Juden und Christen in den ersten Jahrhunderten ihrer Begegnung / Attraction and Repulsion: Jews and Christians in the First Centuries of Their Encounter.* Bilingual ed. Tübingen: Mohr Siebeck, 2015.

————. "Genesis Rabbah's Enoch." In *Genesis Rabbah in Text and Context*, edited by Sarit Kattan Gribetz, David M. Grossberg, Martha Himmelfarb, and Peter Schäfer, 63–80. Tübingen: Mohr Siebeck, 2016.

Schäfer, Peter, and Klaus Herrmann. *Übersetzung der Hekhalot-Literatur.* Vol. 1: §§1–80. Tübingen: Mohr Siebeck, 1995.

Schäfer, Peter, Margarete Schlüter, and Hans Georg von Mutius. *Synopse zur Hekhalot-Literatur.* Tübingen: Mohr Siebeck, 1981.

Schreiner, Josef. *Das 4. Buch Esra. Jüdische Schriften aus hellenistisch-römischer Zeit.* Vol. 5, *Apokalypsen.* Gütersloh: Gütersloher Verlagshaus Gerd Mohn, 1981.

Schremer, Adiel. "Midrash, Theology, and History: Two Powers in Heaven Revisited." *JSJ* 39 (2008): 230–53.

Schwemer, Anna Maria. "Irdischer und himmlischer König. Beobachtungen zur sogenannten David-Apokalypse in Hekhalot Rabbati §§122–126." In *Königsherrschaft Gottes und himmlischer Kult im Judentum, Urchristentum und in der hellenistischen Welt*, edited by Martin Hengel und Anna Maria Schwemer, 309–59. Tübingen: Mohr Siebeck, 1991.

Segal, Alan F. *Two Powers in Heaven: Early Rabbinic Reports about Christianity and Gnosticism.* Leiden: Brill, 1977.

Segal, Michael. "Who Is the 'Son of God' in 4Q246? An Overlooked Example of Early Biblical Interpretation." *DSD* 21 (2014): 289–312.

———. *Dreams, Riddles, and Visions: Textual, Contextual, and Intertextual Approaches to the Book of Daniel*. Berlin: de Gruyter, 2016.

Smith, Jonathan Z. "The Prayer of Joseph." In *Religions in Antiquity: Essays in Memory of Erwin Ramsdell Goodenough*, edited by Jacob Neusner, 253–94. Leiden: Brill, 1968.

———. "Prayer of Joseph." In *The Old Testament Pseudepigrapha*, edited by James H. Charlesworth, 2:699–714. New York: Doubleday, 1985.

Smith, Mark S. *The Origins of Biblical Monotheism: Israel's Polytheistic Background and the Ugaritic Texts*. Oxford: Oxford University Press, 2001.

Smith, Morton. "Two Ascended to Heaven: Jesus and the Author of 4Q491." In *Jesus and the Dead Sea Scrolls*, edited by James H. Charlesworth, 290–301. New York: Doubleday, 1992.

Sokoloff, Michael. *A Dictionary of Jewish Babylonian Aramaic of the Talmudic and Geonic Periods*. Ramat-Gan: Bar Ilan University Press; Baltimore: Johns Hopkins University Press, 2002.

Steck, Odil H. *Israel und das gewaltsame Geschick der Propheten. Untersuchungen zur Überlieferung des deuteronomistischen Geschichtsbildes im Alten Testament, Spätjudentum und Urchristentum*. Neukirchen-Vluyn: Neukirchener Verlag, 1967.

Stone, Michael E. *Features of the Eschatology of IV Ezra*. Atlanta, GA: Scholars Press, 1989.

———. *Fourth Ezra: A Commentary on the Book of Fourth Ezra*. Minneapolis: Fortress Press, 1990.

Teeter, David Andrew, and Bernd U. Schipper, eds. *Wisdom and Torah: The Reception of "Torah" in the Wisdom Literature of the Second Temple Period*. Leiden: Brill, 2013.

Winston, David. *Logos and Mystical Theology in Philo of Alexandria*. Cincinnati, OH: Hebrew Union College Press, 1985.

INDEX

Note: page numbers followed by "n" refer to
numbered endnotes and unnumbered footnotes.

Index compiled by Scott P. Smiley.

thrones and enthronement (*continued*)
and Enoch-Metatron, 109, 114; in
Self-Glorification Hymn, 33–34, 37;
Son of Man and throne of glory,
47–49; suffering servant of God
and, 36; Wisdom and, 27–29
Tigchelaar, Eibert J. C., 43
Timaeus, doctrine of creation in,
151n5
Torah, 9, 30, 56, 69, 72, 77, 108, 119–21
Tosefta, 69
Trinity doctrine, 5
Trisagion ("Holy, holy, holy"), 91, 95,
128–29, 156n37
Trypho, 125
"two powers in heaven" (*shetei
rashuyyot*), 6, 13, 72, 113–14, 116–18,
131, 133
two-sources theory, 145n8

Uriel, 59–60

Wisdom (*hokhmah; sophia*), personified, 25–32, 62

Yehoshua, Rabbi, 131, 164n109
YH epithet, 119, 122, 162n75
YHWH (tetragrammaton), 2–4,
71–72, 77–78, 130, 131, 132–33, 134,
141n4, 148n10, 163nn77 and 88,
164n103; Bavli on "Lord" (YHWH),
124–27; El, Ba'al, and, 3; "Lesser/
Younger YHWH" (*YHWH ha-
qatan*), 13, 110, 113, 136; Moses at the
burning bush and, 132; as term, 2n;
vision of Daniel and, 21–22
Yohanan, Rabbi, 87–89
yored merkavah ("the one who
descends"), 12n
Yose (the Galilean), Rabbi, 82–85, 103,
124

Zutra bar Tuvyah, Rav, 122–24